EDGING TOWARD IBERIA

JEAN DANGLER

Edging toward Iberia

UNIVERSITY OF TORONTO PRESS
Toronto Buffalo London

Toronto Buffalo London
www.utppublishing.com

ISBN978-1-4875-0123-5

Library and Archives Canada Cataloguing in Publication

Dangler, Jean, author
Edging toward Iberia / Jean Dangler.

Includes bibliographical references and index.
ISBN 978-1-4875-0123-5 (cloth)

1. Iberian Peninsula – Antiquities – Historiography.
I. Title.

DP63.D36 2017 936.6′01 C2017-900559-6

University of Toronto Press acknowledges the financial assistance to its publishing program of the Canada Council for the Arts and the Ontario Arts Council, an agency of the Government of Ontario.

Canada Council for the Arts
Conseil des Arts du Canada

Funded by the Government of Canada
Financé par le gouvernement du Canada

Contents

Acknowledgments

Writing this book has been a challenging yet wonderful experience that began in 2005 when Simone Pinet and Óscar Martín invited me to submit an article to a special issue of *diacritics* on theoretical approaches to the study of medieval Iberia. That article, "Edging Toward Iberia," was a more conceptual piece than this book turned out to be, a shift that I explored and developed thanks to recommendations by the anonymous readers at the University of Toronto Press and its Executive Editor Suzanne Rancourt. Between the bookends of the article and this book project, I owe a debt of gratitude to colleagues and audiences who welcomed me for presentations on the project's themes, namely Michael Solomon at the University of Pennsylvania, and Simone Pinet at Cornell University, and Rita Costa Gomes at Towson University for an invitation to participate on a panel at the annual meeting of the American Historical Association. Dialogue with those groups deepened and tested my thinking about non-modern Iberia and its representation.

I truly could not have pursued the various fields of research needed to devise the arguments for this book without the expertise of friends Martha K. Huggins, Malcolm Willison, Edward Snajdr, and Shonna Trinch. Conversations with Alejandro Rupert and Lisa Dillman always enriched my reflection on the project. Grants won through the Georges Lurcy Fund in the School of Liberal Arts at Tulane University were essential to research I conducted at the Biblioteca Islámica (AECID) and the Biblioteca Nacional in Madrid, while Tulane's Research Enhancement Fund and Committee on Research permitted and supported my study of Arabic in Fez, Morocco and Cairo, Egypt. Finally, I am eternally grateful for the love and support in my work and life of my partner, Ainslee Beery, my parents, Edgar W. (deceased) and Nancy J. Dangler, my aunt, Carolyn L. Dangler (deceased), my in-laws, Robert W. and Phyllis L. Beery, and my aunt and uncle, Elizabeth J. and James W. Brunson.

EDGING TOWARD IBERIA

Introduction

Getting a handle on medieval Iberia is no small task. Scholars encounter an array of pitfalls and stumbling blocks in the effort to corral a vast time frame and grasp a complex socio-political landscape of Jewish communities and shifting Islamicate and Hispanicate domains.[1] The challenge of representing this temporal breadth and geopolitical complexity is the broad critical dilemma I address in this book, which proposes ways to envision non-modern Iberia more expansively, rather than as a series of presumably stable kingdoms with defined geographical boundaries. The map by the tenth-century mapmaker Abū Ishāq al-Iṣṭakhrī (fl. 951) that adorns the cover of this book suggests as much, since it indicates a close relation between al-Andalus and North Africa, rather than their vast separation, a difference we will return to in chapter 1. This is what I call "edging toward Iberia," a continual process of assessing the terms and models that guide not only our research but also our critical relationship to the past: how do we conceptualize "medieval Iberia" and imagine the scope of our research before entering the archive or beginning our interpretation and analysis? The choices we make, wittingly or not, about the geographic, temporal, and conceptual frameworks and methods we employ affect our analysis and conclusions. Scholars need new tools and conceptual frameworks in order to avoid biased models such as "the reconquest" or the misnomer "medieval Spain." Instead of relying on a parsed view of the past based on delimited, stand-alone religious or ethnic classifications, the use of interactive frameworks and approaches allows us to edge closer to Iberia's past, which resists facile categorization. Although numerous scholars employ a wide scope in their research, we also struggle to find comprehensive paradigms and methodologies.

This book is divided into three parts: an examination of these problems, a proposed solution using the network theory of Manuel Castells and the World-Systems Analysis (WSA) of Immanuel Wallerstein, and the application of the solution to both new and familiar topics. The first part treats in one chapter critical problems of periodization and geography, and in a second chapter proposed solutions using network theory and WSA. The second part consists of three chapters on networks and systems already familiar to scholars, in trade, travel, and socio-economic relations. In the last section I explore further applications in two new areas, identity and culture, and politics. Network theory and WSA permit the examination of Iberia on a micro scale as a set of interactions between different individuals and groups, while allowing at the same time Iberia's inclusion as an element in macro scale transregional systems. Such an approach necessitates a focus on shifting network links or associations between kingdoms, merchants, or families in non-modern Iberia, rather than on delimited spatial and temporal frameworks. It also compels us to underscore Iberia's profound interaction with global realms, while challenging us to devise nuanced analyses of connections between political spheres, along with varied aspects of non-modern life, such as political events and economic, spiritual, and cultural production and exchange. This approach challenges us to confront a series of assumptions about relations of power in contexts such as feudalism or poverty. Network theory and WSA change the terms that guide scholarship, since medieval Europe no longer retains its conceptual homogeneity and hegemony. Simple divisions between people, languages, discourses, and places become untenable.

Applying the system and network approach to non-modern Iberia is in part an ethical decision to address Eurocentric biases and prejudices in historiography and literary criticism, a decision that necessitates incorporating the ties between al-Andalus and North Africa into larger narratives about non-modern Iberia. Analysing transregional interactions shifts perceptions of Europe as a dominant colonizing agent of history on weaker domains in Africa and the Middle East. In addition, it modifies categorical assessments of the various realms as only either governing or occupied, and casts them instead as mutually dependent, fluctuating historical constructs. Recognizing al-Andalus, Iberia, and the Maghreb as part of the same system is crucial to transforming narratives about medieval Iberian economic and social composition, moving them away from a conventional focus on hierarchies, the reconquest,

Castile's preeminence, and feudalism.[2] Those notions are ineffective as comprehensive, overarching descriptors or frameworks, although each could represent non-modern Iberian conditions at discrete moments and in specific places. Abandoning old paradigms and adopting the network or system allows the integration of al-Andalus in Europe's history and development, in what Ray A. Kea calls the Afro-Eurasian *oikumene* or common civilization, making the Euro-Iberian heritage a true blend.[3] Integrating al-Andalus and Andalusi culture in larger narratives further expands conventional analysis of Hispanicate realms, such as Castile, León, and Aragon.

Using the system or network as a method of analysis illuminates cross-cultural and transregional similarities and contrasts, while yielding a more capacious, transcendent account of non-modern Iberian conditions. It also compels us to be more forthright about our scholarship.[4] Expanding the concept of non-modern Iberia to imagine it both as a part of different systems and a network in and of itself rebuffs a critical reliance on rigid categories and binaries, while requiring a critical engagement with multiplicity, diversity, and shifting positions and values of networked elements.

Theoretical Problems and the Mitigating Solution: Part One

The first chapter presents the main disciplinary problems for scholars in periodization and geographical limits, which lead to the difficulty of finding an adequate name for "medieval Iberia." Researchers have relied on modern concepts of time and place to delimit and define medieval studies since Gaston Paris, Ramón Menéndez Pidal, and other philologists invented the field in the nineteenth and early twentieth centuries.[5] Western elites created medieval studies and used it to ennoble modern nations by identifying national roots in the heroic endeavours recounted in medieval texts, and by contrasting the ostensible barbarism of the past to modern Europe.[6] They founded the discipline on the gaps between time periods and on the innate link between medieval literature and the circumscribed modern polity, engendering biases that have resulted in a range of ill-judged assumptions about non-modern geopolitical conditions, along with the adoption of unsuitable terms, models, and place names to describe the past. This is evident in medieval Iberian studies, where scholars have struggled to find appropriate terminology for their area, often settling on phrases such as "medieval Spain" or "Moorish/Muslim Spain," which denote modern concepts of nations, religion, and geographic borders, rather than medieval political and spatial arrangements.[7]

Iberia's limits and very definition often are indeterminate, resisting any attempt to mould them into modern categories of time and place. Shifting borders and political configurations throughout non-modern Iberia defy monolithic modern national territorial borders or concepts of "Spanish" nationhood and national identity. For instance, the commingling of cultural habits at the court of Enrique IV defy cultural divisions based on presumptions about the separation of geopolitical spheres in "Castilian" Iberia and North Africa:

> During the reign of Enrique IV (1454–1474), the Constable of Castile had been observed at early mass "all got up as a Moor, and very nice too," while at his master's court both French and Bohemian visitors had encountered the Christian monarch guarded by Moorish warriors from Granada (not to mention negroes), clothed and worshipping "in the heathen manner," and seated on the ground with his queen to receive them.[8]

Scholars struggle to describe this political and cultural fluidity without relying on modern concepts of national geographic limits between "Christian" Iberia and the "Muslim" Maghreb. The court of Enrique IV further challenges absolute temporal divisions that would erase Andalusi influence in Castilian territory and regions of governance starting in approximately the thirteenth century.

Persistent historical connections between Iberia and North Africa contest the idea of an early modern break that signalled the disappearance of Muslims from Iberia and the end of relations with North Africa. It is evident that associations continued even after the demise of the Naṣrīd kingdom in 1492 and the expulsion of the *moriscos* in 1609, although Portugal and Spain initiated a dominant colonial relationship rather than a diplomatic one from the late fifteenth century forward, a dominance exemplified by Spain's occupation of Ceuta and Melilla.[9] Even today the bounds of the Spanish state extend to North Africa in Ceuta, Melilla, the Islas Chafarinas (a nature preserve), and Peñón de Alhucemas (a Mediterranean islet), among other territories.[10] Periodization, national and geographic bounds, and the place names they engender prove awkward for scholars seeking to portray historical continuities between Iberia and other regions. These problems are discussed in chapter 1, with full acknowledgment of the struggle faced by scholars seeking to overcome them.

Network theory and WSA are explored in chapter 2 as alternative solutions to the problems of periodization and geography. Scholars in medieval Iberian studies mainly invoke the network concept to describe pilgrimage routes along the Camino de Santiago and the medieval Mediterranean trade networks. Javier Brun, Joaquín Benito, and Pedro Canut called the routes toward Santiago de Compostela a historical network (*una red histórica*) that precedes today's cultural, international circuits, while Olivia Remie Constable relied on the network in her studies on al-Andalus and Mediterranean trade, using it to refer to connections between itineraries, ports, and merchants in the Islamicate commercial system.[11] Neither Brun and his associates nor Constable defined the idea of the network historically, but instead accepted its instrumental, descriptive neutrality, although Brun, Benito, and Canut employed the Camino as an example from the past to show the continuity of networks in the present. Despite descriptions of medieval phenomena as networks or systems, the potential for this imagery in conceptual models of non-modern Iberia has gone largely unexamined. A thorough assessment of the terminology and components necessary to exploring non-modern topics as networks or systems is overdue.

This chapter examines the main principles of network theory and WSA, such as fluid and shifting interactions between central and peripheral elements or nodes in a system, the question of power, and vertical and horizontal network organization, each of which are applicable to non-modern conditions. These principles permit a refocus from a national, categorical, modern world view to an assessment of history and non-modern conditions through the realignments and adjustments in systems which happen over time. They replace the hierarchies implicit in the model of the reconquest, for instance, with a flexibility that permits the exploration of political change through realignments between kingdoms. Network theory and WSA help us to address the problem of periodization by concentrating on rearrangements in long-term systems, rather than absolute temporal divisions between ostensibly different eras.

It is evident that network theory and WSA are rooted in modern technology and the global, capitalist world-system, so their use may seem contradictory given medievalists' traditional avoidance of modern assumptions about the past. Rigid temporal divisions, however, have a tendency to obfuscate rather than illuminate, while network theory and WSA provide methods and tools for analysing the complexity of the past more acutely. What they do not provide, however, are theories of medieval interaction with accompanying arguments to explain network adjustments or historical change, which scholars will continue to devise. At the same time, these methods of analysis complement existing studies by scholars such as Constable, Maribel Fierro, Thomas F. Glick, Eduardo Manzano Moreno, María Rosa Menocal, and María Jesús Viguera Molins, whose work appears throughout this book and whose wide-ranging studies occasionally reference Iberian networks.

The rootedness of WSA and network theory in the modern world-system does not deter scholars (including Oystein S. LaBianca and Sandra Arnold Scham) from employing them as investigative tools that readily lend themselves to links and cross-cultural contact especially in the non-modern Mediterranean milieu.[12] Janet L. Abu-Lughod and Kea have used these models to explore non-modern systems in regions such as Africa and Europe, demonstrating that associations exist on multiple levels ranging from mundane arrangements between merchants to large-scale negotiations between political leaders.[13] Abu-Lughod's and Kea's research offers a guide for integrating network and system principles into studies on non-modern Iberia, and a way to re-establish its constitution through connections and fluid borders, rather than through the anachronistic imposition of rigid geopolitical boundaries.

Scholars increasingly perceive similarities between present and past networks in trade, communication, travel, and economics, and such temporal comparisons are in vogue. However, they often focus on superficial historical resemblance as if networks were intrinsically related or even the same, while failing to acknowledge systemic differences. For instance, Ross E. Dunn points to the roots of modern networks and globalization in the medieval past when he argues that the "dense networks of communication and exchange" described in the *Riḥla* or travel book of Ibn Baṭṭūṭa (b. Tangier, d. 1368) linked virtually everyone in the hemisphere and "exposed the premodern roots of globalization." Similarly, miriam cooke and Bruce B. Lawrence, concentrating on information technology, cast Ibn Baṭṭūṭa as the forerunner and pioneer of Muslim cybernauts and Internet networks.[14] However, modern globalization is far more than mere technological connection, and since Dunn fails to explain "the premodern roots of globalization," his observation leads to doubt about whether those roots were economic and political, as in modern globalization. The lack of depth and specificity is a weakness in cooke and Lawrence's comparison as well. In another problematic conflation, Nayan Chanda contends that the same motivations that drove past events propel globalization today, including "the human search for security and for a better and more fulfilling life," which led people to migrate, trade, try to convert others to their faith, and establish empires, as if the past and the present were cast in the same mould and followed the same pattern.[15] In fact, we will see in chapters 3 and 4 that people did not usually move in the Islamicate trade and travel system for the sake of religious conversion, welfare, and security, but for other reasons.

Scholars of today's globalization also theorize about the relationship between non-modern conditions and the modern system. Many adopt a two-part definition of globalization as a phenomenon that requires temporal contextualization and spatial differentiation, but that is also somehow continuous throughout history. David Held, Anthony McGrew, David Goldblatt, and Jonathan Perraton seem to suggest that globalization is a phenomenon that coheres historically through an organizing logic that is left unexplained. They renounce a telos or evolutionary logic that would link what they call the historical process of globalization, but then they devise a multi-part historical scheme of premodern, early modern, modern, and contemporary globalization, as if it were a phenomenon for all times.[16] Jürgen Osterhammel and Niels P. Petersson recognize that it is problematic to claim that globalization has occurred for thousands of years, yet they also contend that past attempts at globalization, which they seem to define as a desire to move beyond the confines of a village or town, "always broke off at some point," never to be sustained. For this reason, they label the past "the prehistory of globalization," suggesting that modern globalization is the terminus of a series of historical fits and starts.[17] This view of such interaction in the past clearly depends on the iconic idea of the village as homogeneous and universal throughout the medieval world, and as the only possible framework in which to imagine the space of economic relations in the past.

Deeper exploration into the precepts of network theory and WSA in chapter 2 offers alternatives to these descriptions of interaction throughout history and allows scholars to move beyond simplistic comparisons and teleology. Network theory and WSA are indeed germane to non-modern periods because principles of connection and interaction are not inherently "modern" and consequently inaccurate when applied to non-modern people. This is evident in at least one medieval conceptual paradigm about belonging and affiliation in Islamicate domains, as examined below. In Hispanicate kingdoms, however, coherent large-scale schemes are difficult to identify until approximately the twelfth century, when links between Iberian political leaders and northern European realms were increasingly institutionalized through legal and economic structures and the Church. In contrast, non-modern Islamicate realms were organized more generally by a sociopolitical framework akin to a network or system in the corresponding realms of Dār al-ḥarb (the Domain of War) and Dār al-Islām (the Domain of Islam or submission to the will of God). This model dominated in Iberia until the realignment of power relations among kingdoms in approximately the eleventh through thirteenth centuries, when informal Andalusi organizational networks gradually ceded to Hispanicate administrative and religious institutions.[18] The use and meaning of Dār al-ḥarb and Dār al-Islām were regularly negotiated and contested in the past and signified differently than they do today.[19] In the non-modern Islamicate world they constituted organizing principles to connect territories horizontally through the authority of Islamic law. Dār al-Islām consisted of all territories in which "the law of Islam prevails," which until the modern era included the *umma* or Muslim community, along with the rights and protections afforded to the *dhimmī*, Jews, Christians, and Zoroastrians, whose origins in revelation gave them a legitimate place in Dār al-Islām.[20] Dār al-Islām gained its unity through the authority of law, as well as through the *ḥadīth* (the Traditions, or the accounts of what the prophet Muhammad said, did, or tacitly approved of), the latter assuring the protection of the *dhimmī*. Territories outside Dār al-Islām where Muslim law was not enforced were considered Dār al-ḥarb, although there was some agreement that "a country remains dār al-Islām so long as a single provision (*ḥukm*) of the Muslim law is kept in force there." The extent to which the concept Dār al-ḥarb required the hostility of the *umma* has changed over time, since the idea of a holy war during a time of political crisis is "an innovation."[21] Dār al-ḥarb and Dār al-Islām are founded on Muslim law, which depends on the authority of Allāh, who has invested his power in his prophets, particularly Muhammad. The power to enforce laws and promulgate the will of Allāh has been granted historically to Islamic governments, and to a *qāḍī* or judge in an individual legal case.[22] Yet in Umayyad al-Andalus, legal debates about the definitions of the *dhimmī*, along with mutations of the imagined border between the two domains made the relationship between Dār al-ḥarb and Dār al-Islām malleable and shifting. Their relationship resembles the workings of networks and systems because it demonstrates widespread yet changing connections across Islamicate realms, as well as fluctuating links between Muslims and *dhimmī*, or cultural "others."[23] These fluid connections, along with bonds between earthly judges, rulers, and transcendent Allāh were organizing principles in the medieval Islamicate world, and as we will see in chapter 2, they were both horizontal and vertical, like networks and systems, since they referred to lateral links among different territories, and hierarchical connections between human beings and Allāh. Despite the temporal gap between modern network theory, WSA, and the past, the paradigm of Dār al-ḥarb and Dār al-Islām indicates that principles of network connection are not exclusively modern.

Wallerstein recently identified an unresolvable temporal and ideological problem in our capacity to imagine the past through anything but a modern, capitalist lens. He proposed that the national, categorical, modern world view leads to a universalism and a "form of truth" that caused him to question its ability to shed light on "historical alternatives to the endless accumulation of capital."[24] If his pessimism is correct and we are doomed to perceive only the voracious accumulation of capital everywhere in the past, how as twenty-first-century scholars can we imagine historical alternatives to traditional accounts of nonmodern Iberia? This dilemma is why it is important to interrogate our vocabulary, concepts, and categories of analysis. The answer is not to categorically renounce our modern views, which would only solidify a problematic temporal divide between the past and present without getting us closer to the past. Instead, the principles of WSA and network theory serve as inroads to exploring cultural, historical, and literary themes in the humanities and social sciences from a broader perspective.

Application of Methodology: Part Two

The application of network and system tenets to the familiar topics of trade, travel, and socio-economic conditions is taken up in chapters 3 through 5. In addition, and where possible, connections to medieval Iberian literary texts and genres are addressed in order to suggest further applications of network theory to literary and cultural studies. The aim in these chapters is expository and exemplary, rather than exhaustive, and this is reflected in the references to primary works and criticism.

The Islamicate trade system, which spanned the Mediterranean from Iberia and the Maghreb to Yemen and beyond starting in the ninth and tenth centuries, is examined in chapter 3, where Constable's work on the crucial role of al-Andalus and Andalusi traders in the system is highlighted.[25] The most important features of the network are described, demonstrating the application of several of the main principles of network theory and WSA, including the changing status of system nodes, in this case Andalusi ports, and their shifting roles, central and peripheral, in both the small-scale Andalusi network and the larger Islamicate system. Historical changes in the position of al-Andalus itself in the entire Islamicate system are also examined, underscoring the interpretation of historical change through realignments of system elements. This approach abandons the interpretation of non-modern historical change through period shifts and conquest, replacing them with the rearrangement of network nodes. The variable role of al-Andalus in non-modern Islamicate trade epitomizes the idea of medieval Iberia as a series of shifting associations.

A wide range of Jewish, Muslim, and Christian merchants trafficked in the network with largely unfettered movement. They engaged in a variety of partnership agreements in a system that exhibited many market features, such as the distribution of goods based on supply and demand, and for-profit trade among merchants. Yet despite its market characteristics, scholars concur that the Islamicate system operated mainly on principles rooted in social relations, including cooperation, trust, friendship, and reciprocity between merchant partners, and between partners and agents, but which were often bolstered by legal means. In contrast, modern capitalism or globalization is driven by the market principle, which governs the distribution of the means of production, such as land, labour, natural resources, and capital. Karl Polanyi argued that in general, the social component that propels reciprocity in other systems is overshadowed by the demands of the market in the modern system, indicating that pre-industrial economic systems reaffirmed social relations in ways such systems do not in modern industrial capitalism.[26] Integrating the social component of pre-industrial exchange into medieval research requires the examination of modern assumptions about hierarchies at every level of non-modern society.

The difference between the principles of exchange in Islamicate and modern world-systems is important because the socio-economic principle serves as the basis of merchant partnerships in the Islamicate network, and bears out their demonstration of crucial tenets of network theory and WSA. The key roles of reciprocity and trust, which do not predominate in modern capitalism, constitute a departure from the limitations of a presumed vertical-horizontal binary relation among merchant partners, where one ostensibly exercised greater power and control based on assets and prestige, leading hypothetically to vast inequities among associates in trade, as in today's global capitalist world-system. Instead of a categorical or hierarchical organization, merchant partnerships demonstrate that non-modern communities over many centuries and in a vast geographical area were arranged according to socio-economic configurations that diverged from modern assumptions. Scholars' ability to assess non-modern trade and partnerships as based on principles of exchange different from those in the modern global capitalist system is crucial to developing capacious, less biased understandings of the Islamicate network, whose economic and social arrangements ought to be part of our general analytical frameworks for research on medieval Iberia.

The chapter ends with a discussion of the realignment of Islamicate trade in the thirteenth and fourteenth centuries. This realignment accompanied political shifts that generated more dominance-based connections between kingdoms than in the past, as well as a decreasing centrality of merchant partnerships. Armed combat increased in frequency in the Mediterranean, while unobstructed trade waned. Network theory and WSA require that changes in the Islamicate system be assessed through network adjustments, rather than through absolute economic or political subjugations and conquest.

In chapter 4 non-modern travel is investigated with a concentration on the Islamicate travel system, which overlapped in some respects with trade, since both systems traversed the same routes that connected vast transregional territory in Asia, the Middle East, Africa, and Europe. Al-Andalus constituted a nexus of cultural, diplomatic, and economic exchange in the Islamicate system, and was a producer of commercial and cultural products. It was also an essential conduit for the transmission of images, texts, and goods from Baghdad and Damascus to Gaul and northern Europe. The focus here is on the four interrelated activities that predominated in the Islamicate travel system: trade, pilgrimage, travel for intellectual pursuits (*riḥla* or *ṭalab al-'ilm*), and travel for saints' veneration, which paralleled similar journeys in Hispanicate territory. Non-modern travel demonstrates the links between diverse regions, with a series of central and peripheral zones that largely matched those in the trade system. Non-modern people were highly mobile and frequently measured distance not in kilometres or miles, but in differences between "languages and discourses." Rather than crossing national boundaries as in today's modern world, people often took trips close to home, a practice particularly evident in the mostly unhindered

Mediterranean milieu.[27] Travel accounts in Arabic and Romance by Ibn Fadlān, Ibn Baṭṭūṭa, Marco Polo, and a host of others, are renowned for tales of wide-ranging journeys, although Amitov Ghosh argues that travel in the early Middle Ages was so far ranging and constant that it made "the journeys of later medieval travelers, such as Marco Polo and Ibn Baṭṭūṭa, seem unremarkable in comparison."[28] Late medieval journeys may in fact pale in comparison to the early twelfth-century itineraries of the Jewish merchant and scholar, Abū Sa'id Ḥalfōn ben Nathanel ha-Levi al-Dimyātī, who "visited Spain and Morocco as frequently as Aden and India."[29] Joaquín Rubio Tovar shares this view about the openness of the medieval world, asserting that it was continually traversed again and again.[30] This evident mobility contrasts with obsolete, nineteenth-century assumptions about sedentary town life and the isolation of the "medieval village."[31]

In concert with the previous chapter on trade, chapter 4 reveals how non-modern travel dismantles the biased characterization of the medieval world as an unavoidable clash between so-called Muslim and Christian civilizations, and exemplifies instead the porous limits between "Christianity" and "Islam."[32] Both chapters demonstrate that borders and frontiers did not function as they do today, as rigid, national or federal barriers to obstruct passage from outside their realms, or to protect those within their limits. Rather, they functioned fluidly as they do in networks and systems. The fourth chapter also focuses on travellers' intermeshing and cultural exchange in Andalusi and Hispanicate realms, demonstrating the fluidity of Iberian movement and cultural capital. The system of accommodations for merchants and travellers in the Islamicate network serves as a final example of a multicultural, transregional institution that changed in accord with the idea of realigning elements in a system, which in this case were political shifts.

In chapter 5, feudalism, slavery, and poverty are explored as socio-economic conditions which scholars no longer take for granted as transparent in the non-modern world.[33] The application of network and system tenets to these conditions generates findings similar to those in the Islamicate trade system, where vertical, hierarchical interpretations of economic conditions proved insufficient for describing relations among merchants, agents, and polities. In addition, the application challenges assumptions about the similarity between non-modern and modern socio-economic conditions, as in ostensibly universal drives and desires for consumption and wealth, or supposedly "natural" motivation for individual gain. Polanyi's social and economic theories prove useful in revised approaches to these topics as well, since modern assumptions fail to address non-modern enmeshing of economic and social relations.[34] Cross-cultural analysis of the socio-economic organization in Hispanicate and Andalusi realms is employed to demonstrate broader, more enmeshed networked understandings of past conditions than previously possible.[35] A rethinking of the concepts of feudalism, "slavery," and poverty is important not only for enhanced understanding of archival historical material, but also for interpreting people's relationships in other kinds of non-modern texts, such as poetry, short stories, Marian miracles, and hagiography.

Popular perceptions of feudalism frequently cast it as a simplistic hierarchical relation between land-owning lords and impoverished vassals, although scholarly reinterpretations are increasingly well known, especially with regard to medieval Iberia. The reassessment in this chapter explores feudalism by contrasting the presence of feudal relations in Hispanicate domains with their absence in Andalusi realms, as proposed by historians such as Glick and Miquel Barceló.[36] Following their lead, the system model is applied to feudal relations in Hispanicate domains in order to analyse their historical shifts through the expected modifications in networks and systems. Tenets of network theory and WSA, which call for the assessment of vertical and horizontal arrangements and the role of power, complement scholarly revisions that demonstrate Iberian feudalism's complexity and variability. It is further proposed that Iberian feudalism be studied as an interconnected system of economic and social values and relations that shifted over time.

Scholarly reassessments of non-modern "slavery" and poverty are not as well known and require more background development. Suppositions about the hypothetical vertical order of non-modern economic and social relationships continue to inform common ideas about non-modern "slavery," to the extent that it tends to be equated with the system of modern chattel slavery that burgeoned with the transatlantic slave trade starting in the fifteenth century. Despite scholars' common reference to "slavery" in al-Andalus and the Islamicate world-system, discussions about what the term means continue to be rare. The increase in the transfer of sub-Saharan labour to al-Andalus with the rise of the Almoravids in the eleventh century was not comparable to the transatlantic slave trade that began in the fifteenth century.[37] Historians have long acknowledged that "slave" trafficking was a major type of trade that connected Africa, al-Andalus, and Europe in the medieval

Mediterranean milieu. However, the differences between non-modern and modern systems of exchange are crucial in recognizing the vast gap between non-modern and modern "slavery." A number of historians have noted the complications that arise in using terms such as "slave" and "slavery" in a medieval context, arguing for recognition of different meanings of non-modern and modern enslavement.

Network theory and WSA can help bring precision to the concept of non-modern "slavery," a term that continues to be used indiscriminately to characterize a wide range of socio-economic relationships. For instance, in Moses I. Finley's study of ancient servitude, he claimed that the wage laborer only came into being with the rise of modern capitalism, while workers in the ancient world figured in a labour continuum that included enslaved people as well as "other types of compulsory labour." Finley averred that scholars have relied on a series of ill-fitting categories to describe slavery in the ancient world, owing to what he called the "bad state" of historical and sociological efforts to classify labour.[38] Consequently, labour is discussed in this chapter within the framework of a continuum or system, rather than being compartmentalized in a series of delimited universal categories, such as "slavery."

Like "slavery," poverty does not have a transhistorical meaning, despite stereotypes and assumptions about its stability and ubiquity through time. Scrutinizing the interpretation of non-modern poverty and wealth helps to avoid assumptions about similarities between medieval impoverishment and the considerable poverty that characterizes the modern capitalist world-system.[39] This scrutiny also has important repercussions for the study of poor people and impoverishment in a variety of non-modern discourses, found in literary, legal, and medical texts. Many factors contribute to theories about medieval destitution, including modern progress narratives about a chronological trajectory of human betterment from the deprived past to the luxuriant present, and the tendency of systemic modern poverty to contribute to skewed views of the past. If individual profit and the accumulation of goods were not universal goals in non-modern exchange, as Polanyi argues, then many questions remain about penury and the distribution of resources in the non-modern world.

Non-modern privation is difficult to assess, since it is a vague term that differed across time and place. Indeed, the persistent lack of data prompts sweeping generalizations about "medieval poverty" or "the medieval poor," which are inconclusive for understanding socio-economic distribution in discrete communities. The problem of periodization weighs heavily on this issue, since the vast temporal and geographic realms of "the Middle Ages" often aggravate the imprecision of undiscerning statements. People with limited economic means were certainly part of non-modern societies, though documentation varies broadly and definitions are equivocal.[40] Scholars sometimes recognize different kinds of medieval poverty, though data is often scant or non-existent.[41] Here, non-modern "poverty" in Iberia is evaluated as a system in which social, economic, and political reordering affected the definition and development of impoverishment over time. The comparison and contrast between Andalusi and Hispanicate realms further illuminates the varying conditions of non-modern Iberian destitution and its constant relational quality.

In the section on feudalism there is a discussion of the literary repercussions that result from this reassessment of socio-economic conditions in the reading of the *Cantar de mío Cid*. A broader treatment of repercussions in other literary genres, such as hagiography and devotional literature, is not included here. Cross-regional connections implicit in networks and systems permit new links between the socio-economic organization in Iberian hagiography and saint veneration in the two traditional sites of Palestine and North Africa.[42] Medievalists often research Marian miracles and hagiography in Castilian or Galician-Portuguese alongside literary and spiritual models from France, although links to the south and east would likely enhance findings about socio-economic themes. Our perception and analysis change when we connect medieval Iberia simultaneously to intellectual centres inside and outside Europe, such as eleventh-century Gaul, England, and Qayrawān (Tunisia), a linkage that yields important information about the circulation of texts, knowledge, and goods.

New Themes: Part Three

New themes for future application of network theory and WSA are explored in two chapters in part three. In chapter 6 it is seen that the models reframe ideas about non-modern politics and the idea of the polity, which historians at times have treated according to modern geographic and social divisions, including geopolitical separations of power. This is nowhere more evident than in the concept of the Iberian reconquest as a religious and political battle between Christians and Muslims. Rather than to continue deploying this obsolete model, it is better to characterize non-modern Iberian politics as networks and systems whose centres and peripheries, or polities and locales consistently realigned and readjusted over time. This approach dislodges scholars' emphasis on religion as the chief reason for political and social change and assigns it a complementary role among a variety of factors. Network theory and WSA emphasize broad, transregional connections, a polycentric formation, different types of political realms, and shifting relations between them. This perspective centres on politics and political change as a result of pacts, adjustments, and associations between domains, rather than unquestioned, top-down relations of power or crushing militarism, as will be seen in this chapter.

Although Christians began to consolidate their power in 1085 with the capture of Toledo, and then again in 1212 with their victory at Las Navas de Tolosa, a more fortified "Spanish" nation-state only began to develop in the late fifteenth century with the homogenizing efforts of the Catholic Kings (1469–1516). The Jewish and Muslim expulsions and conversions from 1492 on constituted part of the effort toward religious and cultural hegemony by the Castilian-Aragonese Crown, even though such uniformity was only achieved over the following two to three centuries. Benedict Anderson's idea of the modern nation as an imagined community not only applies to nation-states of the nineteenth and twentieth centuries, but also to non-modern Spain under the Catholic monarchs and the subsequent Hapsburg dynasty, which struggled to achieve social and political homogeneity.[43] This series of shifts is surveyed in this chapter, not through the lens of the triumphant reconquest, or the watershed year of 1492, but as realignments of political realms and interests. The view of non-modern Iberian politics as a struggle between Christianity and Islam, or between east and west, is thus challenged.[44]

In chapter 7 the application of network theory and WSA to non-modern Iberian individual and collective identity is explored. System and network fluidity require that identity be considered through shifting affiliations, rather than through essential corporeal qualities or naturalized qualities of character. In the same way that modern theories of subjectivity commonly link individual identity to processes of identification, as in Judith Butler's concept of gender as malleable, so non-modern subjectivity consists of changing qualities and desires.[45] The question of collective identity is explored as an Iberian system of interconnected communities, Andalusis, Asturians, and Castilians, that cohered through their interactions. The chapter includes a discussion of the understanding of the identity system over time, citing the case of Andalusi Muslims who converted in the sixteenth century, and an application of network and system tenets to demonstrate such shifts through adjustments in the Iberian identity system. This long networked view considers Iberian identity through varied links in a continuum, displacing modern tendencies to transpose national and ethnic categories into the past. It is further demonstrated how network theory and WSA reduce dependence on other modern categories, such as religion, destabilizing a patently mythical master narrative about the European origins of Spanish history and identity in the Visigoths, through the lineage of Pelayo.[46] Instead of relying on the idea of a static Spanish identity derived from Germanic tribes, the network framework corroborates Américo Castro's claim about Spain's complex genealogy and identity: to be Spanish today is to derive from a range of backgrounds, such as Iberian, Carthaginian, Greek, Roman, Jewish, Visigoth, Berber, and Arab.[47]

The chapter ends with an assessment of culture using network and system principles and Glick's model of what he called the dominant cultural polarity. The discussion focuses on Andalusi and Hispanicate culture as an interconnected network with continuities and divergences, and draws in topics from previous chapters, including pilgrimage and *ḥajj*. The argument is made that pilgrimage and *ḥajj* ought to be explored as nodes in the same non-modern travel and pilgrimage system, a decision with ramifications for collective and individual identities in separate Andalusi and Hispanicate realms, and in the Iberian domain more broadly speaking.

PART ONE

Fundamental Problems; Models and Methods

Chapter One

Periodization and Geography

Periodization and geography are fundamental problems in medieval studies with no simple solutions, despite increased critical attention to the limitations they impose. They underpin traditional concepts applied to medieval Iberia, including the reconquest and the view of medieval history as a religious battle, which although recently reassessed and critiqued, continue to appear in scholarly publications as unquestioned.[1] The perennial difficulties of periodization and geography must be acknowledged and addressed so that network theory and World-Systems Analysis (WSA) may produce more even-handed results.

Periodization

The artificial periodization of the Middle Ages into a ten-century time frame from 500 to 1500 CE, nestled neatly between so-called antiquity and the Renaissance, is a well-known invented paradigm. Iberianists often diverge and choose another fiction using the year 1492 to mark the end of the Middle Ages and the beginning of Spain's imperial and literary "Golden Age," a break that Barbara Fuchs recently denounced as arbitrary and inaccurate.[2] The important events of 1492 did not bring about the absolute socio-political and epistemological shifts implied in the logic of periodization, as Fuchs demonstrates in her discussion of Spain's persistent *maurophilia*.

Periodization consists of dividing time into convenient blocks, even though people do not typically live their lives as if they were aware of passing from one momentous era to another. This is evident in the way medieval people envisioned their relation to antiquity, a relation marked by continuity and simultaneity, in contrast to the perception of radical differences between epochs that characterize modern views.[3] Medieval people also represented time as cyclical and providential, demonstrated by the scribal teams of king Alfonso X (1253–84) in their prologues to the manuscripts of the *Estoria de Espanna* and the *General estoria*, where time so described was used as a political strategy to illustrate the inevitability of Alfonso's imperial ambitions.[4] Yet despite this evidence of political motivation in the medieval description of time, modern critics more generally have used the idea of time as cyclical and preordained by God to reify the medieval past as devoutly religious, in contrast to secular modernity. Kathleen Davis examined the prejudices and political consequences of this medieval/modern divide in her exploration of sovereignty and the revelation of a skewed view of historical transition as being from an ostensibly medieval and "feudal" ecclesiastical order to a modern urban state fuelled by commerce.[5]

Scholars such as Davis indicate that the creation and delimitation of the Middle Ages wholly depends on the equally skewed construction of the modern, a critical perspective that entails imposing a set of values from the present on the past. According to Margreta de Grazia, the medieval/modern divide is "less a historical marker than a massive value judgment" that grants relevance and legitimacy to anything "modern," and irrelevance to anything prior to the determined modern moment, whenever it may be.[6] The prejudices of periodization are evident in progress narratives in culture and history, which José Antonio Maravall examined starting in the sixteenth and seventeenth centuries. From a progressivist perspective, history is seen as permitting the incremental growth of humankind in successive periods that often culminate in the nineteenth century with the victorious liberal state, following eighteenth-century efforts to unify and homogenize Spain through the consolidation of *fueros* or regional legal codes.[7] The biases and political consequences of periodization evident in this type of progress narrative are at work as well in traditional scholarship on the Middle Ages dealing with topics ranging from ethnicity, hierarchies of powerful and marginalized groups, to gender relations, nationhood, and authorship and book production in medieval manuscript culture. Scholars including Norman F. Cantor, John Dagenais, Umberto Eco, Mark D. Meyerson, and Gabrielle M. Spiegel have identified many modern presumptions and values erroneously applied to the past.[8] For instance, Dagenais rebuked modern critics for applying the values of book culture to non-modern manuscript production, citing the modern focus on the author rather than on the reader's primary role in manuscript culture, and pointing out as well the failure of modern methods to allow for variation among medieval manuscripts of the same work. In another example, Meyerson argued for more nuanced explorations of tensions of power in medieval Iberia when he questioned the application of marginalization and otherness to Muslims and Jews, who were central to Iberian cultural and political life and often not at all othered or disempowered. Despite scholars' acknowledgment of these biases in criticism and historical writing, periodization continues to be difficult to resolve or avoid, and while the most useful scholarship refrains from the unthinking application of modern concepts to non-modern periods, scholars are always hampered by their own limits and values, even if they wish to describe the past with some accuracy.

Accordingly, suggestions for overcoming periodization's hurdles are both instructive and useful. Kathleen Davis and Nadia Altschul posit a solution to its biases in the shifts that may occur when scholars from "colonies and emerging nations" consider what medieval and the Middle Ages mean, especially when they condemn empire or debunk "the world-historical status of medieval/modern periodization." These new points of view may combat the entwined relationship that Davis theorizes elsewhere between the "Middle Ages" and colonialism, demonstrated by critics' attribution of ostensibly superstitious practices to the medieval population and the parallel fashion in which colonial subjects were depicted in the sixteenth century.[9] Ania Loomba recommends that researchers adopt an inquisitive rather than an empirical mode in approaching their work, questioning what they do instead of setting out to find absolute solutions. She argues that crossing geographical and temporal boundaries is, "first and foremost, a conceptual exercise, which involves, to paraphrase Chekhov, the correct formulation of a question, rather than the necessary finding of an answer."[10] Jennifer Summit and David Wallace propose collaboration as a remedy for spanning chronological and geographical limits.[11]

Other scholars recommend continued reassessment of critical or descriptive terms, as emphasized by Daniel Martin Varisco in his critique of the prejudiced, erroneous application of "medieval" and the "Middle Ages" to the Islamicate world, as well as to India, China, Japan, and Jewish history.[12] Varisco's critique centres less on the contrast between "medieval" and "modern" and more on the biases inherent in the terms "medieval" and the "Middle Ages." He traces the roots of the term "medieval" to sixteenth-century Europe and the 1000-year timeline of the "Middle Ages" to events in Christian history, claiming that both distort Islamicate history and create an image of time that does not correspond to historical events. Varisco does not advocate for a thorough disavowal of these terms, but proposes more finely tuned terminology used "in a manner that does not efface the Muslims whose history we study." Suggested revisions include relying on specific centuries and dates instead of terms for general periods, although Varisco himself opts for the standard "caliphate" when referring to the timespan covered by the Umayyad and 'Abbāsid dynasties.[13]

It is clear that scholars will never be perfectionists in this regard, nor will they ever devise flawless substitutes for the terms currently in use. Umberto Eco proposed three decades ago that to some extent we always recast the "Middle Ages" in our contemporary image, which manifests in our novels, movies, and scholarship. The modern is always in the medieval, and the medieval in the modern, however they may be construed. Eco drew attention to the constructed quality of the past by delineating ten types of "Middle Ages" made popular today through media and scholarship; two of the more recognizable include "the Middle Ages as a barbaric age," and "the Middle Ages ... of occult philosophy."[14] Yet even when we recognize periodization's snares and the weighted biases attached to "medieval" and "Middle Ages," it is difficult to characterize or study a moment, event, or person in the tenth or eleventh century in a way that demonstrates only the values of that time rather than today's, or to describe the past "on its own terms" or "for its own sake," in the words of Simon R. Doubleday.[15] This effort is plainly impossible. Nonetheless, attention to the biases inherent in terms and names is a step toward greater acknowledgment of the values they imply in scholarship. In addition, the increased use of a number of more expansive terms related to our field offer better descriptive flexibility, terms such as "Islamicate" and "Andalusi," which, following Varisco's suggestion, begin to reduce dependence on "medieval" and the "Middle Ages."

José Rabasa offers the idea of the "non-modern" to temper or replace biases of "medieval" and "Middle Ages." "Non-modern" directly challenges three problems of periodization: it avoids the strained identification of the years 1492 or 1500 to divide the medieval and early modern periods; it brings into relief the implied teleology of the term "pre-modern," as if "the modern" were the inevitable terminus of "the pre-modern"; and third, it avoids the marginalizing of non-European cultures, histories, and experiences that fall outside the categories of the "medieval" and "early modern," as in the Caribbean, Latin America, and Asia.[16] The non-modern wholly sets itself apart from the modern, rather than positioning itself before the modern, as in pre- or early modern. Rabasa contends that the modern refers to "a periodizing construct" or "a rupture" with the past which is construed as medieval and shaped as retrograde, outdated, and incompatible with the modern. He explores the coexistence of temporal realities, suggesting that the non-modern and the modern sometimes coexist, as among indigenous peoples in Mexico today. The idea of the non-modern implies that by focusing more on the quality of an event, concept, memory, or thing, rather than on its circumscription in time, scholars may avoid the teleology of the term premodern and thus gain better insight into historical shifts and cultural practices.

Rabasa's approach resonates with the method of Manuel De Landa in his fascinating work *A Thousand Years of Nonlinear History*, published in 1997. De Landa calls his book a "philosophical meditation on the historical processes that have affected ... energetic, genetic, and linguistic" materials. He argues that his book is a meditation on "the history of matter-energy [composed of 'rocks and winds, germs and words'] in its different forms and of the multiple coexistences and interactions of these forms."[17] Perhaps De Landa's way of conceiving history is similar to Rabasa's in his observations about the non-modern as occurring simultaneously with the modern, and that what matters is the way in which different forms interact, rather than the supposedly inevitable march of time with momentous events and human progress. Although these ideas and practices have far-ranging implications for important shifts in our scholarship, the coexistence of the modern and the non-modern may also unintentionally result in collapsing phenomena (De Landa's concept of forms that constitute matter-energy) so that the past resembles the present, and vice versa, when in many ways they are vastly different.[18] The conflation of phenomena from the past and the present is another way that the treatment of the question of time may be problematic in our work, as noted in the introduction, when a supposed likeness between non-modern and modern networks is observed, as in discussions of globalization, or of trade, communication, and travel systems.

Greater attention must be paid to the relationship between the past and the present, as it has clear implications for our scholarship. While people today often use the present to inform the past, medieval people tended to study the past in order to make it part of themselves and inform the present. María Rosa Menocal pointed out that non-modern people thought the past instructed them on how to read, see, and understand in their present time, a key reason for the assiduous focus on memory in the Middle Ages.[19] Kathleen Biddick presents the problem in another way when she rejects a paradigm of history based on the categorical division of what she dubs "that was then, this is now," as if the temporal contrast were so certain. Biddick defines history not according to empirical "facts" or events, but through our involvement with "that was then," "this is now," with how we create their relation: "history is precisely the way we are implicated in the 'that was then,' 'this is now.'"[20] Edging toward Iberia always entails the meeting of the past and the present because we never completely divest ourselves of modern paradigms and values. If, as Menocal observed, time is fluid, nonlinear, and overlapping in our reading and writing practice – "What reader, what writer, has ever read within an ordered history, much less written as part of it?"[21] – then perhaps the strategies suggested above, along with updated methods and models will contribute to helping foster a more expansive scholarly production about the non-modern world.

Geography and Its Attachment to Place Names

Just as "medieval" and "Middle Ages" depend on the collective understanding of the artifice of periodization, so too "medieval Spain," "medieval Iberia," and other names require tacit agreement about the geographic and political limits of our field. However, it is difficult to know what we mean by non-modern "Spain," which denotes a modern nation-state whose geographical borders include the peninsula's Pyrenees and coasts, while also extending to the Balearic and Canary Islands, and to Ceuta, Melilla, and other territorial claims in North Africa. Moreover, few of us become proficient in all the languages of non-modern Iberia, including Arabic, Hebrew, Latin, and the romance languages, nor would any scholar have sufficient time and knowledge to conduct research about all of the Iberian manuscript communities in such a vast space and time. These limitations suggest that "non-modern Iberia" is an ambitious name for our field.

Geography proves to be a poor referent for our place names and terms because it did not serve as a political or cultural boundary in non-modern eras. For instance, the Pyrenees mark Spain's northern territorial and political limit today, an idea that scholars sometimes transfer to the past in reference to the frontier space of the so-called Spanish March, or the *marca hispánica*. This term designates the area around the Pyrenees that fell to Frankish control from 780 to 801 and bordered al-Andalus, although it is unclear where the zone began and ended.[22] It is possible that the Pyrenees may designate the territorial border between Iberia and Gaul, or between Muslims and Christians in non-modern periods, though the mountains were deceptive "as any kind of stable line."[23] Battles and skirmishes between Andalusi and Frankish troops continued well into the ninth century and did not end (as popularly believed) with the eighth-century Muslim defeat at the battles of Tours or Poitiers. Between approximately 935 and 950 Andalusis established a permanent base at Freinet (Farajshīnīt/Jabal al-Qilāl) near Saint-Tropez on the coast of Provence,[24] while relations between al-Andalus and Carolingian realms in the eighth and ninth centuries saw everything from diplomacy to rancor and battles, to Andalusi settlements in Narbonne. Muslim geographers such as al-Bakrī (eleventh century, b. Huelva) and al-Ḥimyarī (fifteenth century) positioned Narbonne along the northern border of al-Andalus, a limit considered much farther north than most historians acknowledge.[25] This history raises serious doubt about the Pyrenees as a demarcation between the "Christian north" and the "Muslim south."

Until approximately the fourteenth century, geography did not denote strict limits of political power. For instance, in the late third century CE under the Roman leader Diocletian, the *diocesis Hispaniarum* was not confined to the Iberian Peninsula, but also included the administrative and military units of "Mauritania Tingitana" in North Africa.[26] In the seventh century, the theologian Isidore of Seville underscored the relationship between the peninsula and North Africa when he stated that Hispania included the North African province of Tingitania.[27] For much of the Middle Ages, North Africa and Iberia were intimately connected politically and economically as the western-most regions of the Islamicate empire. The tenth-century mapmaker Abū Ishāq al-Iṣṭakhrī (fl. 951) regarded Iberia and North Africa not as separate units, but as comprising the single entity of al-Andalus, a concept contained in the non-modern meaning of the Maghreb.[28] Today Maghreb in Arabic means "where the sun sets" or the occident, and is also the name for Morocco. However, it once referred to the western portion of the Islamicate empire and may have reached from Iberia's Ebro Valley region to the limits of Egypt, thus comprising al-Andalus and all of North Africa.[29] Even names regarded as stable in meaning, such as al-Andalus, fluctuated with the vicissitudes of history and time. Manuela Marín asserts that "the Andalusi reality" was always geographically variable and represented decreasing territorial power from the eleventh century on.[30]

It has been difficult to capture this vast and variable territorial extension with the names we use for non-modern Iberia. Spain and *España* are no more consistent in meaning or referent than al-Andalus. Non-modern chronicles and texts such as Alfonso X's historical prose, the *Cancionero general de París*, Juan de Flores's *Triunfo de amor*, and Isidore's translated *Crónica* and *Historia de los godos* referred to the romance variants *Espanya*, *Espanna*, and *Hispania*, although scholars today often regard *España medieval* and "medieval Spain" as anachronistic and narrow in scope when designating medieval Iberia as a whole. During the early years of Hispanicate expansion variants of *España* designated for Christians the Islamicate territory of al-Andalus and only later came to refer to the entire peninsula.[31] In contrast, Arab historians sometimes called Hispanicate Iberia *Ishbaniya*, although they also used the term *al-Andalus* to refer to the full peninsula, or only to Islamicate territory.[32] Maravall argued for a constant knowledge of *España* on the part of historiographers starting with Isidore of Seville and continuing through the chronicles of, among others, Sancho III el Mayor, Alfonso VI, Alfonso I el Batallador, Alfonso VII, and Alfonso X. Maravall understood *España* as a dynamic and changing concept, shifting from an early focus on the lives of kings to the emphasis on the link between *España* and the common people.[33] Yet he also sought cohesion in the use of the term, as in the following definition:

> Spain is, for our medieval historians, a human entity located in a territory that defines and characterizes it, and to which something happens in common, an entire history of its own.[34]

Although Maravall did not define *España* as a modern nation, and in fact at one point deemed the concept an abstraction, he seemed intent on linking medieval people to "the Land," *España*, and thus to the idea of a common community throughout the Middle Ages.[35] This common, essential thread that would connect a group of people over many centuries is dubious, due to political vicissitudes, migrations, and shifts in the meaning of *España*.

"Iberia" generally denotes the geographic peninsula with coastal borders and limits in the Pyrenees, as attested by Isidore of Seville in the *Etimologías*, where the name is derived from the Ebro River (*río*

Ibero) and refers to the peninsula before its denomination as *Hispania*.[36] Many use it today because it never denoted a bordered political state, although it fails to capture the peninsula's profound historical, political, economic, and cultural connections with North Africa, Europe, and the Middle East, precisely because it was not used in this way. The term is best understood as a theoretical concept that designates a variable space of interaction between different groups of people, rather than a bordered, static geographical space.[37]

The frontier is another term related to geography, but useful for wresting the concept of non-modern Iberia from the borders of the modern state and from physical circumscription by the Pyrenees and at its coasts. The frontier has evolved since historians linked it to the Iberian reconquest as a space between Muslim and Christian military forces, or as a site of Christian conquest.[38] Now, scholars such as Peter Linehan argue for the frontier's fluidity and frequent lack of definition. Linehan rejected the notion of "frontier behavior" as either reinforcing the goals of crusade or of *convivencia* (cohabitation), arguing instead that the medieval Iberian frontier permitted both, since it was the space where the "inconsistencies of human behavior" were played out.[39] In medieval Iberian studies it often denotes a society without strict limits, borders, or categories of knowledge and identity, a valuable starting point for rethinking non-modern borders and spatial boundaries, and for envisioning medieval Iberia in fluid, unbound ways.[40] Many scholars agree that the frontier usually was a vast zone and not a line:

> A fronteira podia, portanto, ser, em muitos casos, um espaço bastante largo e não uma linha. (Therefore, the frontier could be, in many cases, a rather wide space and not a line).[41]

The frontier had different meanings over time as a border, an edge, a space of conflict and cohabitation, though never a line.

Linehan and Eduardo Manzano Moreno extend the idea of frontier from Iberia to the whole of medieval Europe, which they indicate constituted a frontier space lacking both a stable social order and strict borders between political realms. Linehan also asks, however, if medieval Europe was entirely frontier, where was "the European hinterland or metropolis?"[42] Where were the urban centres and the marginal, rural areas? In response to these questions, it may be that the frontier cannot be understood as the edge of "the European hinterland or metropolis," but as a conceptual, unfixed space. Indeed, perhaps we cannot conceive of defined zones and hinterlands at all in non-modern history, if as Ronnie Ellenblum argues fluid "centres" should replace the border as a determinant medieval quality.[43] While Ellenblum acknowledges that fixed borders were not part of the medieval spatial organization, instead of describing non-modern society as a frontier he contends that medieval political communities "were more easily characterized by their centres or by their common association with a ruler than by their physical space."[44] Ellenblum maintains that central areas had spheres around them with boundaries, though it is difficult to determine "well-defined zones" because those boundaries were mutable and changing. According to Ellenblum, scholars should focus on "spheres of various degrees of influence," rather than on bordered political zones.[45] We will see in chapter 6 that these fluid ideas of geography began to yield to notions of more rigid geographical limits beginning approximately in the thirteenth century.

The concept of network and system connections further assists in imagining Iberia not through the limitations of geography, but as a series of varying political and cultural links in a system among peoples of the peninsula and nearby regions. The idea casts non-modern Iberia not as an enclosed geographic or temporal space, nor even merely as a series of shifting kingdoms, but rather, as a network of interrelated attachments between varying individuals and groups. The idea of associations extends Iberia from geographical and temporal boundaries to a series of cultural, economic, or political relationships. If we recognize medieval Iberia not as a peninsular terrain bounded by the Pyrenees, the Atlantic, and the Mediterranean, but as a series of associations between its people and communities throughout the Mediterranean and Europe, then we shift our focus from geopolitical domains to dealings among communities. Surely at times it is necessary and appropriate to investigate and describe non-modern Iberia according to political boundaries and geographical limits, but often their imposition does not serve research efforts or yield a deeper understanding of the past. Just as many critical theorists (from Gilles Deleuze and Félix Guattari to Eve Kosofsky Sedgwick) have emphasized an understanding of the human body through constantly shifting attachments to other people and things, rather than according to supposedly inert qualities and absolute characteristics, so too may we study medieval Iberia in relation to its varying alliances with other regions and political realms, and not as a straightforward geographical area.[46]

Network associations and the fluid border or frontier make plain the idea that edging toward Iberia is edging toward Africa and the Middle East at the same time. These techniques help to create a broader concept of non-modern Iberia, the Mediterranean, and the larger non-modern world that transposes medievalists' traditional point of reference from Castile and repositions it in various places and times according to scholars' objectives. As pivotal components of network theory and World-Systems Analysis, these techniques are useful tools for thinking about geography and time in new ways, and for interpreting culture and history more broadly. Network theory and WSA provide alternatives not only to categorical conceptions of non-modern Iberia, but also to straightforward, clear-cut perspectives on historical and political change. They open avenues to the weighted problems of geography and periodization and invite more expansive ways to imagine Iberian history than through the conventional temporal gap wrought by the events of 1492, with the medieval period on one side and the "Golden Age" and the ensuing march to modernity on the other.

Chapter Two

Network Theory and World-Systems Analysis

Network theory as conceived by Manuel Castells and World-Systems Analysis (WSA) as devised by Immanuel Wallerstein provide conceptual frameworks and models for examining non-modern interaction at different levels of connection, whether local and quotidian, or regional and occasional. Relying on the tenets of these theories highlights interactions in the past between regions that have often been regarded as separate, such as Iberia, North Africa, and the Middle East.

A Larger Framework: Network Organization

Researchers consider the network a model of organization that has existed for a very long time, although scholars of modern globalization and information systems have largely theorized and defined it, most notably the renowned sociologist Manuel Castells.[1] Many of Castells's ideas lend themselves to the non-modern fluidity of the border or frontier and shifting associations between individuals and realms, while others are more difficult to link to the past. Castells defines the network as a series of decentralized, interconnected nodes that are adaptable and flexible rather than fixed and static.[2] Nodes are significant in a system not for their inherent characteristics or qualities, but because of their contributions to the network's goals. Castells argues that as the involvement of a node weakens, networks tend to reconfigure themselves by possibly relinquishing and adding nodes.[3] He maintains that network organization consists of horizontal relations between nodes, in contrast to the vertical hierarchies that scholars often used in the past to describe society's structure.[4]

Castells argues that networks constitute "the fundamental pattern of life, of all kinds of life," indicating their ubiquitous presence across time.[5] The network's permanence as a paradigm of cultural organization has led Javier Brun, Joaquín Benito, and Pedro Canut to call historical networks such as the Camino de Santiago precursors to modern cultural networks in globalization, and harbingers of their future success. They argue that the network's horizontal, decentralized structure holds great promise for the achievements of cultural networks today, such as African Books Collective, Afrilivres, CARIBNET, and Red Cultural Mercosur, which seek to resolve inequities and social problems around the world.[6] Other scholars, including Oystein S. LaBianca, Sandra Arnold Scham, and "students of the past including historians, archaeologists, social anthropologists and political scientists who take the long view" of history, perceive in the past many of the same organizing patterns and phenomena as those Castells has noted.[7] In particular, they mention pervasive past trends, such as "networks dependent on new technology, identity versus collectivization issues, and globalization itself."[8]

Despite LaBianca's and Arnold Scham's reliance on the ideas of Castells in theorizing and historicizing the idea of the network, and in contrast to Castells's own claims about the network's pervasiveness in time, Castells's research has always focused on modern phenomena, including the Internet, information technology, and communication systems. Yet in publications of 2006 and 2009, he examines the relation between non-modern and modern networks, expressing scepticism in 2006 about wholesale efforts to apply his ideas to non-modern eras. While Castells does not oppose the attempt, he critiques the effort to devise "a unifying social theory ... in which networks, identities, and their relationships would be key elements to anchor our understanding." In his view, the network cannot be applied indiscriminately and anachronistically as "a unifying social theory" across time. Castells maintains that he did not intend to conceive "a general theory of society" in his work; rather, he wanted "to understand the dynamic nucleus of our evolving, contemporary social structure, and the processes of social change related to it."[9] Castells insists on constantly identifying the historical contexts and social conditions that produce networks in different eras.[10] He argues that starting in approximately the 1970s innovations in information and communication technologies differentiated networks from prior times and defined the dominant, contemporary technological paradigm he dubs *informationalism* or the Information Age. People shaped this paradigm through enhanced ability in information processing and knowledge production, which was facilitated by innovations in microelectronics and genetic engineering.[11] The importance of modern innovations in information and communication technologies in Castells's network theory makes it apparent why he insists on the rootedness of his work in the present, without a connection to networks in the past.

Although Castells is right to insist on the relevance of his work in the contemporary age of informationalism, rather than in all historical periods, comparing his ideas to non-modern conditions indeed produces insight about both the past and the present, along with the relationship between them. LaBianca and Arnold Scham contend that Castells explains human phenomena and trends that researchers also identify in the past, though he devises an innovative theoretical framework for present rather than past conditions.[12]

Three essential features characterize Castells's framework and analysis, which offer potential contributions to non-modern studies. The first feature is the relation of power to the network's horizontal or vertical makeup, although Castells's theories in this regard are difficult to resolve in medieval systems. Castells argues that networks are primarily horizontal rather than vertical, which seems an accurate assessment of non-modern networks by and large. Yet he also maintains that scholars in the past often erred in describing ancient and medieval systems as vertically arranged with the control of power always residing with society's elites, who were legitimized by mythology and religion. Castells reproves the ethnocentrism and apology that often led scholars to this hierarchical paradigm, with its "one-directional flow of control and command" from powerful elites downward. However, he also attributes this biased depiction to the strength and greater capacity of the vertical structure over the network, which he asserts, prevailed historically because of technological limitations that permitted the downward flow of communication from institutions that were vertically organized. The lack of rapid technology in the past permitted elites to control the flow of information and goods, effectively making networks subordinated extensions of institutional power:

> Under such conditions, networks were an extension of power concentrated at the top of the vertical organizations that shaped the history of

> humankind: states, religious apparatuses, war lords, armies, bureaucracies, and their subordinates in charge of production, trade, and culture.[13]

Castells claims that the evolution of communication technologies increasingly allowed networks to become more independent from power centres, as with the advent of the industrial revolution. Railways and the telegraph constituted the infrastructure that produced what Castells calls "a quasi-global network of communication with self-configuring capacity."[14]

It is difficult to reconcile Castells's simultaneous recrimination of and agreement with scholars who interpreted non-modern networks as vertically structured. While suggesting they erred, he also asserts that networks were vertically ordered before certain technologies made network organization more horizontal. Castells's explanation for the shift from vertical to horizontal organization is also tricky, since his contrast of technological limits in the past to technological innovation in the modern world fails to consider the relative impact of technological invention in any given age. LaBianca and Arnold Scham point out that past innovations in communication technologies were as significant in their time as they are in the modern world.[15] If as William J. Mitchell suggests, the development of information and communication technologies throughout history is motivated by the desire to expand and augment the human body and mind, as in the explosion of wireless and portable computing devices in the twenty-first century, then their value derives from their discrete context, and not from their comparison to succeeding inventions.[16] Castells's comments about the verticality of non-modern networks are unpersuasive because models for describing medieval space and order, namely, the variable medieval frontier and spheres of influence, indicate that power in the Middle Ages was often diffuse rather than solely centralized in "vertical" authorities or institutions. The extent to which elites such as medieval religious and secular authorities consolidated power and maintained full control over networks, as Castells maintains, varied considerably in non-modern eras. Furthermore, although medieval and modern global networks clearly differ, it is difficult to imagine that systems in the past were more controlled "vertically" by powerful elites than they are in today's neoliberal, free-market, corporate-political system. It is also doubtful that the most important political and economic "nodes" today, such as New York or ExxonMobil, are more autonomous and horizontally ordered than non-modern nodes in the past, including Cordova, Toledo, or Cluny.

The question of horizontal or vertical network organization is one of Castells's thorniest topics, since his arguments leave many questions and doubts about the concentration of power and its effects, along with the supposed role of modern technology in establishing categorical differences between non-modern and modern systems. In his more recent work of 2009, Castells largely shifts the focus from the spatial horizontal/vertical configuration to a more nuanced discussion of control based in part on David Singh Grewal's ideas about power in networks today. Although Castells's latest discussions about power are in my opinion better suited for networks in the present than in the past, Singh Grewal's theories about network power are suggestive for non-modern systems. Singh Grewal does not identify technology as decisive in modern networks, but indicates instead that technological innovation in any age may bring people together in a network, since technology facilitates social relations.[17] He argues that social cooperation and coordination adhere in a network by way of certain standards that network participants share, such as a common language or a particular ideal. He does not view power dimensionally as vertical or horizontal, but as created through the standards that constitute social coordination. The more the standards are used, the more powerful the network becomes, to the extent that the system resists innovations in the standards so as not to disrupt the accepted flow of social cooperation. Standards are double-edged because they both permit cooperation and inhibit novelty: "Inherent in the use of any standard is a tension between the cooperation that it allows users to enjoy and the check on innovation that it also imposes, since innovation would constitute a break in an ongoing cooperative regime."[18] Thus, Singh Grewal suggests that network power may appear simultaneously and paradoxically vertical and horizontal, since it can be imposed vertically and coercively, yet also manifest horizontally in people's freely made choices.

In non-modern eras, the vertical/horizontal network duality also emerges in Islamicate regions in the organizing principles of Dār al-ḥarb and Dār al-Islām, which demonstrate what Singh Grewal identifies as the embrace of standards by a community, in this case the authority of Islamic law and its promulgators, as well as the *ḥadīth* (teachings of the prophet Muhammad), which assured the protection of the non-Muslim *dhimmī*. Dār al-ḥarb and Dār al-Islām also show the duality that

Singh Grewal describes in the vertical, perhaps coercive, quality of network connection through authoritative Islamic law and government, which bestowed on leaders the authority of Allāh, in addition to the system's horizontal inclusiveness of non-Muslims and even in some cases of territories not dominated by Islamic law. The complex power relations that Singh Grewal describes in modern networks are implicit in the medieval understanding of Dār al-ḥarb and Dār al-Islām, indicating that power sometimes functioned consistently in non-modern and modern systems.

In addition to the idea of vertical or horizontal organization, Castells proposes a second network feature in the "space of flows," which is "the non-substantial dimension in which information is transmitted and transactions conducted."[19] He maintains that most major functions in today's network society occur in this way, without synchronicity or contiguity, as in banking, finance, and media systems.[20] While Castells's characterization of "space of flows" depends on technological innovations that allow for asynchronous, virtual communication and interaction, LaBianca and Arnold Scham argue that the non-substantial dimension in which they take place was prefigured by ancient and medieval trade routes likely present from the initial stages of human history. They point to the simultaneous exchange of goods and ideas that occurred along those routes and emphasize their "ripple effect" far beyond the place of physical trade. They also contend that an innovation such as the domestication of pack animals could be as meaningful in the past as information technology in the present for facilitating a non-substantial dimension of exchange. LaBianca and Arnold Scham demonstrate that many of the same processes of trade, movement, and social organization that Castells imagines in the present are found in the past, albeit in different forms: "the corporate and national 'tyranny' of flows that is implicit in globalization processes today are not new."[21] Although networks and wide-ranging connections between different peoples certainly existed in the past, LaBianca and Arnold Scham could argue further to expose temporal differences between modern and non-modern interactions. They seem to hesitate to fully expose historical differences between non-modern flows and movement in contemporary globalization, perhaps in an effort to dignify the past as equally complex and sophisticated as the present. They fail to mention that the associations and flows that predominate in today's global economic networks differ considerably from associations in medieval trade networks. The absence of this kind of discussion in their work obscures important historical differences between medieval and modern systems.

The third main feature of Castells's network frame is the role of the nation-state, which did not exist in the Middle Ages as it does in modern periods. Political spheres of influence predominated in the past over delimited polities, thus potentially constituting nodes with crucial network roles, such as the Andalusi ports that functioned as economic centres. Although fluid, non-modern arrangements seem to have little connection to the idea of the modern state, they also coincided in some ways. Castells's concept of the modern network largely depends on the dissolution of the state and its borders, although he also recognizes its continued struggle to achieve political legitimacy. Castells describes the state in modern globalization as a node in a specific "political, institutional, and military network" that converges with other networks to forge "social practice." Other networks include the international institutional system composed of organizations such as the United Nations, the World Bank, the World Trade Organization (WTO), the International Monetary Fund (IMF), and the International Criminal Court.[22] Castells proposes a new model of the state, which he calls "the emerging network state," characterized by the sovereignty and authority shared "between different states and levels of government," the flexibility of government operations, and the variety of times and spaces of interaction between government entities and citizens. These characteristics have a number of consequences, including the obscuring of political representation and the alienation of citizens from the political process.[23]

Castells maintains that states operate differently now in globalization than they did for much of the twentieth century, as evidenced by their interactions with international institutional networks, including influential multinational corporations and their agents, such as the IMF, the World Bank, and the WTO. These new associations have produced a crisis of legitimacy and state identity, since states strive to conform to the old, nearly obsolete model of the nation-state as rigidly bordered and self-serving.[24] Singh Grewal concurs with these changes in state configuration and operation when he highlights fractured state sovereignty in their current commercial dealings according to the conventions of the WTO:

> The world's nations, driven by extrinsic reasons (if nothing else) now conduct their commercial intercourse according to its conventions [the WTO's]. Thus, understood in the language of sociability and sovereignty, the WTO represents a highly developed form of global sociability that now performs some of the functions – and thus holds some of the power – that were formerly in the control of national sovereignties. National sovereignty has thus been fractured, with what formerly constituted its full power now divided among many bodies, only some of which are national representative bodies, such as parliaments.[25]

However, at the same time that Singh Grewal and Castells underscore the crisis of the state today, both scholars demonstrate its paradox in globalization. Singh Grewal declares that all aspects of social relations have globalized except politics, which continues to be dominated by the idea of the self-governing nation-state and its presumably autonomous decision-making authority.[26] Castells illustrates this paradox in the tension between the emerging network state and the highly popular yet outdated notion of the bordered, sovereign nation. This idea of the nation may be antiquated, although Castells demonstrates its traction in the self-serving way in which countries interact in global networks. Instead of working toward the network's collective good, state authorities negotiate in order to leverage as much gain as possible for themselves, a dynamic that Castells insists will continue to lead to the rise of nationalism and the revival of national sovereignty.[27] He demonstrates that the state operates today in two ways, first as a polity whose delimited borders and sovereignty function as powerful markers of citizen identity in national politics, and second, as a shifting node in a series of overlapping networks, which causes the state to lose its consistency and force as a perceived autonomous entity. Thus, while the importance of the nation-state has declined in modern networks, the idea of the integral nation with its supposedly fixed boundaries continues to be crucial in certain political settings, as for instance, in the politics of migration, immigration, commerce, and travel.

Castells's idea of the modern state as an "emerging network" resembles the concept of medieval spheres of influence in its flexibility and malleability, perhaps leading LaBianca and Arnold Scham to observe the similarity between non-modern networks and the flows of modern globalization. Yet at the same time, the nationalist self-interest of the modern state does not readily apply to medieval polities, which LaBianca and Arnold Scham do not overtly acknowledge. Instead, they demonstrate important resemblances between non-modern and modern networks, thereby debunking ideas about modern preeminence and innovation over an unsophisticated past. Recognizing differences between modern and non-modern networks would bring into greater relief the divergent values or standards implicit in their organization. The gap between the demarcated modern nation and the fluid medieval polity is one such crucial variation.

Network theory provides a framework for interrogating conditions in medieval Iberia, including vertical and horizontal arrangements, the role of technology, collective and individual identities, conditions of exchange, regulations in commerce and travel, and the organization and function of political realms. World-Systems Analysis offers another, more comprehensive framework for similar inquiries about non-modern Iberia and trade, travel, and socio-economic systems. In contrast to the recent attention paid to Castells and network theory by scholars of the past, researchers such as Janet Abu-Lughod, Enrique D. Dussel, and Ray A. Kea have relied on Wallerstein's work and WSA since at least the late 1980s in studies on historical systems. The history and main components of WSA, along with its use in those studies, lay the groundwork for the examination of how network and system principles pertain to the medieval Islamicate trade and travel systems, and to Iberian socio-economic arrangements.

A Larger Framework: World-Systems Analysis

Immanuel Wallerstein devised World-Systems Theory in 1974 with the publication of *The Modern World System I: Capitalist Agriculture and the Origins of the European World-Economy in the Sixteenth Century*, though he currently prefers the term World-Systems Analysis. Academics largely favour World-Systems Analysis to World-Systems Theory because it designates a model for investigative purposes that permits the incorporation of many individual theories, rather than denoting a theory that intends to prove something.[28] Starting in the 1970s, world-systems analysts investigated interactions between many geographic places and among diverse realms of social life, including the economic and the political, in an effort to broadly explain the modern capitalist world-system that originated, according to Wallerstein, in the sixteenth century.[29] WSA was founded on two core principles, that communities (or societies) do not exist in isolation, and that "societal trends follow cycles or patterns."[30] P. Nick Kardulias argues that WSA differs from other frameworks of interaction in its broad geographical scope, its emphasis on systems as hierarchical, especially with regard to economics, and often in scholars' attempts to account for long-term patterns of expansion and contraction in systems.[31] WSA occasionally overlaps with Castells's network theory, although ultimately they focus on different phenomena. Castells identifies information technology as the catalyst of the development of modern, free-market globalization, and as the mechanism that differentiates modern networks from systems before approximately the nineteenth century. Wallerstein does not deny technology's importance in the modern world, though he refutes its fundamental role in the creation of what Castells and others regard as the novel system of globalization. For Wallerstein and proponents of WSA, the opening of markets in today's globalization has occurred in cycles since the development of the modern world-system in the sixteenth century.[32] While network theory and WSA diverge on certain points, they coincide on others, as in their attention to economic and social hierarchies.

Although WSA is more comprehensive than network theory, Castells did not set out to examine as far-reaching a temporal scale as Wallerstein. Instead, both scholars devised their frameworks to address different scopes. While Castells meant to explain processes of change in today's social structure, Wallerstein proposed an analysis of the entire modern capitalist world-system. WSA emerged from the confluence of several theoretical innovations, which included the notion of core-periphery as developed by the United Nations Economic Commission for Latin America (ECLA), the subsequent invention of dependency theory by theorists such as Fernando Henrique Cardoso and Endo Faletto, and debates about "total history" and what Wallerstein calls "the triumph of the Annales school of historiography in France and then in many other parts of the world."[33] The concept of core/periphery was an essential component of WSA in positing, simply, that all partners were not equal in relations of economic trade. Stronger countries became known as the core, while weaker nations were dubbed the periphery. In the 1960s, core/periphery theorists maintained that inequalities could be remedied if periphery states developed mechanisms to eradicate unequal trade relationships, a simplistic formulation that overlooked many details, including political influence in economic dealings. In their succeeding investigations, dependency theorists analysed the convergence of the political and the economic in particular.[34]

The Annales approach to history greatly contributed to shaping WSA with its emphasis on the profound, systematic study of historical phenomena, rather than on what could be uncovered in the archive, on work carried out in disciplinary isolation, or on the concept of history according to national units created from modern nation-states. The historian Fernand Braudel was notable in this regard, particularly due to his criticism of superficial historiography as the narration of episodic events, and of the idea of history as founded on eternal truths. Instead, Braudel proposed that long-lasting basic structures underpinned historical systems, and that cyclical processes such as expansions and contractions in economic systems guided those structures.[35] Braudel's ideas continue to influence scholarship, as evidenced by contrasting concepts that historians continue to employ in "the long view" of historical inquiry known as the *longue durée*, a study over a long period, and research focused on a shorter timeframe. Braudel is especially renowned for his research on the sixteenth-century Mediterranean as a world-economy.[36]

Despite the longevity of world-systems theory and WSA, Wallerstein continues to clarify and revise his ideas, such as the meaning of "world" in hyphenated terms including world-system and world-economy. He never intended the hyphen to designate a system composed of the whole world, but rather meant for it to refer to a system that was a world in itself:

> This is a key initial concept to grasp. It says that in world-systems we are dealing with a spatial/temporal zone which cuts across many political and cultural units, one that represents an integrated zone of activity and institutions which obey certain systemic rules.[37]

Although scholars of non-modern periods have used WSA's framework mostly to examine political and economic topics, researchers of modern periods have been more inclined to extend the model to the humanities. Literary scholars have studied contemporary "world literature" for the last several decades, and a recent volume edited by David Palumbo-Liu, Bruce Robbins, and Nirvana Tanoukhi explores WSA in the humanities.[38]

WSA has already been used to analyse non-modern systems, unlike network theory, which scholars have only recently examined in relation to non-modern networks. A clear beginning was made with the work of Abu-Lughod in 1989, who used the principles of WSA to study Europe's rise as an economic force between 1250 and 1350 amid the medieval world-economies of Asia, North Africa, and the Middle East. Her book was novel because it showed that Europe was peripheral rather than central to world trade prior to approximately 1300. Abu-Lughod identified eight interlinking regional subsystems from the Mediterranean to the South China Sea that were connected by sea routes, rivers, and overland roads. Each subsystem had a number of centres or nodes, or what Abu-Lughod called "world cities," which were mostly ports. The eight subsystems formed a world system in which direct trade between faraway regional centres was difficult due to the limits of technology. Consequently, the central nodes served as exchange points for commercial goods in transit to far-off markets. Abu-Lughod declared that the subsystems were more self-sufficient and less dependent on one another than subsystems today because manufacture and assembly were contained within a region and not sent to subsystems beyond.[39] Oddly she failed to address the breadth of the medieval Islamicate world-system and thereby elided al-Andalus and Iberia from her analysis, generally giving North Africa short shrift.

Abu-Lughod critiqued Braudel (whom she otherwise praised) for failing to explicitly situate Europe's development from the eleventh to thirteenth century within the abovementioned pre-established world-economies.[40] In addition, she demonstrated that Europe's supremacy by the sixteenth century over eastern economies was not due to any unique feature or internal superiority on its part, but to the east's "temporary disarray."[41] In other words, as Olivia Remie Constable noted, the rise of one place or region in any particular time was not due to its superiority, but to changes in the larger world-system.[42] Abu-Lughod's work refuted and rendered obsolete the idea that Europe was pre-eminent throughout history, from the remote past to the present, and instead contended that it became increasingly dominant in the early modern period. Aside from her perplexing neglect of al-Andalus and North Africa, Abu-Lughod reinforced sophisticated medieval world-systems in Asia, Africa, and the Middle East that researchers often disregarded, a perspective that ran counter to common scholarly beliefs, such as the ostensible uniqueness of Italy's role in the Mediterranean trade system with the rise of Genoa and other kingdoms from the fourteenth century.[43]

Other aspects of Abu-Lughod's use of WSA are instructive for how we might employ it in the future to revise analyses of the past. For instance, she refused to engage in a number of what she deemed "fruitless" discussions about the "origins" of modern capitalism and the supposed temporal boundary between "traditional world-economies" and "a modern world system," preferring instead to investigate "the seamless web" of the economic system that preceded Europe's ascendancy.[44] Much like LaBianca and Arnold Scham's rebuke of Castells's claim about the unique role of information technology in the modern network, Abu-Lughod refuted attempts to identify a particular moment of change from a "traditional" to a "modern" economy. In one rebuttal to such temporal parsing, she cited Braudel's analysis of the economy of thirteenth-century Italy, which he claimed exhibited the necessary characteristics, including capitalist institutions and "industrial production, using free wage labor," to categorize it as "a capitalist world-economy."[45] Italy's capitalist status in the thirteenth century thus countered scholars' efforts to identify a temporal break between "traditional" or non-capitalist economies of the medieval past and capitalist systems in the present. However, in Abu-Lughod's view, absolute temporal distinctions were neither easy to confirm nor the most compelling questions to ask about non-modern world-systems.[46]

Enrique D. Dussel offered a slightly different interpretation of Europe's rise than Abu-Lughod. Dussel maintained that Europe has exercised hegemony over the world-system for approximately the last 200 rather than 500 years, since indigenous and eastern cultures continued to wield sufficient authority to preclude Europe's domination in the sixteenth through eighteenth centuries. Although Dussel recognized their waning predominance in the early modern period, he also viewed the past as important in assessing their re-emergence today "from beyond the horizon of European modernity" as a return to the world-system stage.[47] Dussel thus created a temporal link between the present and past that was characterized by both continuity and shifts in the role of indigenous and eastern cultures in the world-system. He demonstrated that examining the past through the interactions of networks or world-systems not only displaces Europe's assumed dominance, but also provides a broader interpretation of conditions in the present, as in the relationship between the former strength of eastern and indigenous cultures, and their contemporary resurgence.

Another example of WSA's application to non-modern periods is Kea's compelling article on the world-system of the western Sūdān from 1200/1000 BCE to 1200/1250 CE. Kea focused on the historical phases of its urban, cultural, socio-economic, and political formation and relied on archaeological findings to characterize the western Sūdān as a world-system with trading centres in Kawkaw/Gao, Tadmakka, Koumbi Saleh, and Tegdaoust/Awdaghast. He sought to cast it as "a historically dynamic part" of the Afro-Eurasian *oikumene*, or common civilization, and to counter established scholarship that failed to recognize the Sahara as an historical region worthy of integration.[48] Instead, Kea argued that traditional scholarship relied on the essentialist notion of "sub-Saharan Africa" as an undifferentiated zone, portraying it as a space where nothing happened with any historical importance. Kea's analysis directly relates to our interest in associations in the Islamicate trade network, where al-Andalus was patently linked to western Sūdān, most notably through the Maghribi scholar-traders called the Kharijites, who were already highly active in the eighth century and continued to trade during the rise of the Almoravids in the eleventh and twelfth centuries.[49]

Kea defined a world-system in the following way, arguing that its features were evident in four core zones that comprised the world-system of the western Sūdān:

> A world-system can be defined as a trans-regional, polycentric formation comprised of interaction networks, urban-based settlement hierarchies, different kinds of political domains and regimes of surplus accumulation, economic zones, production networks, social and geographical divisions of labor, cultural spheres, and markets.[50]

Kea described the western Sudanese world-system according to spatial, political, and cultural dimensions, as in the urban centres that developed in one core zone, the floodplain regions of the valleys in pre-thirteenth-century Middle Niger and Senegal. These towns constituted dominant nodes of commerce and trade and their presence coincided with the expansion of outlying hinterland communities that reinforced economic activity in the urban centres through specialized trades. The hinterland communities were subordinated to the more dominant centres, thus showing the hierarchical spatial and social dimension that marks WSA. Kea examined the shifts in this model during the period of Islamicate ascendancy in the seventh and eighth century CE, when Muslim merchants formed towns devoted to the administration of economic trade.[51]

Kea further incorporated the temporal idea of cycles in his analysis, another important facet of WSA. He linked variables such as political changes, population shifts, climate, environment, and modifications in trade to demonstrate cycles of growth/expansion and crisis/contraction and their effects on the world-system. Kea vindicated western Sūdān's participation in the development of the Afro-Eurasian *oikumene* by demonstrating its key role in the diffusion not only of gold and other commodities to Europe and the Middle East, but also of scholarly work by intellectuals such as Ibn Rushd.[52] Kea showed that WSA contributed to a deeper understanding of western Sūdān's history in general, and to its incorporation into the larger framework of a common Afro-Eurasian legacy and culture.

The general features of World-Systems Analysis definitely characterize the research of Abu-Lughod, Dussel, and Kea, such as interaction among stratified groups in a system, the ideas of core/periphery, scale of analysis, whether macro, medium, or micro (local), and the long- or short-term temporal frame. Their work further demonstrates WSA's value as a paradigm of analysis rather than a theory of interaction or of causation in history. Richard E. Lee maintains that Wallerstein himself insisted that WSA "has always been an interpretive approach or perspective," rather than a theory to prove or to show causality in world events.[53] In a recent volume on WSA's application to research during the Bronze Age, scholars implicitly concur in WSA's ideal use as an analytical, explanatory model rather than a theory, since they consider it insufficient for explaining social change or causation.[54] Several of Wallerstein's ideas have been routinely criticized over the years, such as his insistence on WSA's ability to explain almost any historical event, a claim that fails to take into account "voluntary acts" by individuals or groups of people, or the top-down focus of the core/periphery dynamic, which often leaves little room for people's agency on the margins.[55] In order to incorporate important historical acts by individuals and groups into a discussion of WSA, Palumbo-Liu, Robbins, and Tanoukhi propose thinking about Wallerstein's paradigm less as a system and more as a history with complex contingency, arguing that casting WSA in this light "would involve scaling back somewhat our sense of his [Wallerstein's] ambition."[56]

Despite its limitations, WSA is a useful tool for thinking about non-modern Iberia in a more intricate way – as a series of shifting associations with other realms. Network theory and WSA suggest that we abandon inert, simple binaries, such as static notions of centres and peripheries, and instead examine relationships in culture and history as always shifting and in flux.

PART TWO

Application of Methodology: Trade, Travel, and Socio-economic Conditions

Chapter Three

The Islamicate Trade Network

The non-modern Islamicate world-system exhibited many of the network characteristics devised by Manuel Castells and the world-systems features described by Immanuel Wallerstein and Ray A. Kea. It constituted a world in itself composed of a series of spatial and temporal regions that included primarily Iberia, North Africa, and the Middle East, with links to India, Asia, the Sahara, and western Sūdān. It thus traversed a broad swathe of political and cultural spheres with no region existing in isolation. Scholars describe the network as a free trade zone and a "medieval common market," where Jewish, Muslim, and Christian merchants travelled and exchanged without barriers.[1] Partnerships between traders and their agents were one of the system's most important defining features, leading Avner Greif to call the trafficking by Jewish merchants "free, private, and competitive," as demonstrated by the eleventh- and twelfth-century documents found at the *geniza* or depository at the synagogue in Fusṭāṭ or Old Cairo. Customs were normally imposed at seaports, but Mediterranean traders generally enjoyed unobstructed travel and trafficking of goods.[2] Thomas F. Glick calls the camaraderie and associations between merchants of different faiths throughout the system the tangible expression of the Muslim belief that "there is blessing in movement (*fī'l-ḥaraka baraka*)," a conviction that extends beyond the world of commerce even to this day.[3]

Al-Andalus was a core component of the Islamicate trade network from the tenth to the fifteenth century, serving as a hub of cultural, diplomatic, and economic exchange among people from diverse regions. It was also an essential conduit for the transmission of images, texts, and goods from Baghdad and Damascus to Gaul and northern Europe. Olivia Remie Constable contended that al-Andalus played a crucial role in three main ways before the realignment of Mediterranean commerce among Islamicate and European merchants and kingdoms, which began approximately in the fourteenth century: it was an axis of multiple trade routes; its geographic position allowed it to benefit from and perhaps manipulate this trade; and it was a producer and consumer of commercial goods. Traders exchanged a wide variety of products whose importance fluctuated over time. Many Andalusi goods were produced and sold or exchanged throughout the Islamicate world: olive oil, silk, linen, cumin, cordoban leather, copper, and mercury; Glick characterizes the role of al-Andalus in the world-system chiefly as an exporter of goods.[4]

Andalusi trade took place mainly at its ports, including, among others, Valencia, Almería, Denia, and Málaga, and Seville provided important access to the Atlantic. Constable maintained that merchants from the Islamicate world and southern Europe usually reached al-Andalus by sea, although evidence also demonstrates overland trade with northern Iberian kingdoms. The shipping channel between the peninsula and the Balearic Islands was essential to the circulation of Islamicate and eventually European vessels.[5] Commerce to and from al-Andalus passed through what are now Tunisian cities and towns, especially Qayrawān and its closest port, al-Mahdiyya, although movement shifted east to Alexandria with the Hilālī invasions of North Africa in the mid-eleventh century.[6]

The Maghreb was both a market for Andalusi goods, as well as a region of transit and transport, since North African ports were the primary points of contact between al-Andalus and the larger Islamicate network. Merchants and travellers sailed the short distance across the Straits of Gibraltar from Algeciras to Ceuta, where they either continued on to other ports or connected to Maghribi caravan routes that carried travellers and merchandise through Qayrawān to Damascus and Baghdad, and back again. The poet from Granada, Ibn Mālik (1163–1249) observed that on a clear day one could see Ceuta from Algeciras, the shortest possible voyage between the two shores, which took only one day. The transfer of goods from Algeciras to Ceuta meant that Andalusi traders directly participated in the Mediterranean network even during the winter when open sea travel often was impossible.[7]

Andalusi travel and trade routes by sea and caravan demonstrate the general system tenets in the links between a wide range of geographic regions and diverse peoples from Europe, Africa, and the Middle East. Andalusi merchants sometimes built bases in Sicily or Tunis (Ifrīqiya), which were middle points between al-Andalus and the east. Documents from the ninth century on attest to trade between merchants from al-Andalus, Syria, Iraq, Egypt, and Aden.[8] Many Andalusi merchants trafficked abroad, as demonstrated by the Andalusi merchant colony in Tripoli, mentioned by the traveller and geographer Ibn Ḥawqal (b. tenth century, in Nisibis, southeast Turkey). There are records also of the merchant-scholar 'Abd Allāh B. Massara (b. 882) who travelled with his brother to trade in the Near East, and the merchant-scholar Abū Bakr Muḥammad b. Mu'āwiya al-Marwānī (d. 968) who earned 30,000 dinars trading in the markets of Iraq and India, only to lose it all in a shipwreck on his return to al-Andalus.[9] Travel and economic exchange extended into Asia as gold from Africa moved east via Egypt into Asia, while Asian silk and spices were transported west to al-Andalus and the Maghreb.[10] Gold passed through Egypt to its final destination in India as compensation for the silk and spices desired by Mediterranean merchants, who purchased these luxuries to sell in the west.[11] Al-Andalus was also a conduit for trade and travel to northern realms. Philippe Sénac maintains that Gaul and eastern North Africa were in contact from as early as the eighth and ninth centuries through the Jewish merchants known as the Rādhānites, whose itineraries took them from Gaul and al-Andalus to Sūs al-Aqsā, a town near modern Tangier, Ifrīqiya (Tunisia), and Egypt. The Rādhānites also traded extensively in India and China, further evidence of the shared, interconnected histories of east and west, of Damascus, Baghdad, Qayrawān, Cordova, al-Andalus, Zaragoza, Gaul, Timbuktu, and the Sūdān.[12]

Al-Andalus further serves to illustrate the network precept of changes in nodes, and the system tenet about shifts in central and peripheral zones, manifested in alterations in the relative importance of Andalusi ports, along with the transforming role of al-Andalus itself in the larger Islamicate world-system. Shifts in the status of Andalusi ports and the nature of trafficked goods often occurred as a result of changes in the system elsewhere or in conjunction with political alterations closer to home in Iberia or the Maghreb. For instance, Umayyad leaders from the eighth through the early eleventh centuries were keen on international maritime trade, and this is demonstrated by documentation about port administration, shipyards, and taxation, as well as construction of a number of new cities built specifically as mercantile centres in the late ninth and tenth centuries, such as Pechina/Almería, Asilah (Morocco), and Tenes (Chlef province, Algeria). This new construction bolstered the traditional connection between cities and commerce in the non-modern Islamicate world.[13] Ibn Ḥawqal visited al-Andalus twice during this period in 948 and 974/975, and observed that all Andalusi cities were famous for their markets and shops, referring especially to markets in Caracuel, Calatrava, Gharra, and the frontier city of Guadalajara; he noted also the availability of costly goods from faraway places, such as woollen fabrics (*aṣ-ṣūf*), beautiful and expensive Armenian velvet, and high-quality tapestries.[14] In contrast to the Umayyads, succeeding *ṭā'ifa* rulers were usually more interested in their own affairs, with the exception of Ibn Mujāhid (1044–75) of Denia, although later Almohad and Almoravid rulers were solidly involved with the administration of trade. The Almohads especially sought to control access to their sea ports, as demonstrated by a treaty with Pisa in 1186 that permitted trade in only four North African ports and banned access to all Iberian ports except Almería, where Pisan ships could dock only for emergency repairs and not for trade. Increased political tension with northern Iberian kingdoms provoked heightened Almohad control in the late twelfth century.[15] Political, demographic, and economic changes occurred in the broader eleventh- and twelfth-century Islamicate system, which shifted influence among Islamicate realms, and increasingly, among Islamicate and European kingdoms. For instance, political changes in the Maghreb during the eleventh and twelfth centuries with the rise of the Almoravids and Almohads, along with the emergence of the Fāṭimīd dynasty in Cairo, demonstrate shifts in the relative importance of political centres. This is illustrated in the move from Cordova – the centre under the Umayyads – to Marrakech, Fez, and Seville under the Almoravids and Almohads. Constable particularly underscored changes in the eleventh century, such as the Fāṭimīd move from the central Maghreb to Egypt, raids conducted by nomadic tribes in Ifrīqiya, as in the Hilālī invasions mentioned above, and Norman incursions in the south central Mediterranean.[16] Political adjustments in al-Andalus and the Islamicate world-system generated shifts in the importance of Andalusi and North African ports in trading activity, shown in the change from the small number of key ports in the tenth century under the Umayyads, to the expanded number in single *ṭā'ifa* kingdoms thereafter, thus confirming Castells's description of the network as a system of decentralized, impermanent, shifting nodes.[17] The network image is useful as well for describing the changing influence of ports during the realignment of Mediterranean commerce among Islamicate, Hispanicate, and Italian kingdoms.

Discussions of vertical and horizontal social, political, and economic organization in network theory and WSA make valuable, apposite contributions to understanding the relationship between the Islamicate trade system and al-Andalus, which appears vertically organized in some respects and horizontally ordered in others. While many agree that merchants encountered few barriers in the Islamicate world-system, the relative absence of authoritative, vertical hurdles was compensated for by the imposition of local restrictions that international merchants expected to find abroad. Regulation of commerce and trade varied among local rulers, who relied on the aid of government bureaucrats and *sharīʿa* law, although laws governing commerce responded to merchants' practical needs and were not beholden to narrow sacred legal notions.[18] In the documents of the Cairo Geniza, Islamic and Jewish law about commercial contracts and partner agreements was often similar, especially since legal scribes of both faiths frequently took great care in crafting rules that would be acceptable to Jewish and Muslim jurists of different legal factions.[19] Local officials sometimes established controls on a reciprocal basis, such as taxation, depending on the rules created by leaders in other regions.[20] Abraham L. Udovitch contended that authorities and rulers enacted arbitrary policies that affected trade, although Constable observed that regulations and taxes were similar across al-Andalus despite some variation in controls and levies. Hence, Constable indicated similarities in Andalusi controls, in contrast to Udovitch's suggestion of diverse regulations more generally in the Islamicate system. What seemed to fluctuate at times in al-Andalus were details of control, such as amounts of tolls and taxes, rather than significant discrepancies among Andalusi ports, as in rules about the storage of goods or accommodations in merchant hostelries called *fanādiq*.[21]

In al-Andalus, the interest and direct intervention of government officials in commerce and trade depended on the period and type of ruler, from the express concern of Umayyad leaders to the declining interest of succeeding *ṭāʾifa* rulers, and later to the sustained attention to trade of Almohad and Almoravid leaders. Government involvement varied depending on the motives behind regulation, which ranged from a desire for control over the admission of certain foods to official or personal economic gain.[22] Andalusi governors sometimes owned individual boats or entire fleets for shipping, which they leased to merchants according to contracts that were highly regulated by law. For instance, ʿAlī Ibn Mujāhid of Denia (1044–75) owned at least one ship that he leased, and a number of documents refer to its commercial voyages between Denia and Egypt.[23] Constable demonstrated that for the most part Andalusi government officials were not concerned with commerce as an abstract concept, but instead sought to manage the individual components of trade, including "ports, merchants, markets, hostelries, ships, goods, and especially taxes." International traders encountered local regulations established by regional governors in different ports. Government officials, such as the military governor called the *qā'id* and the local market inspector known as the *muḥtasib* or the *ṣāḥib al-sūq*, monitored local trafficking.[24] Constable stated that a foreign merchant acknowledged such authority in individual areas of his transactions, such as taxes on his goods or housing at a port, but "not as overall control of his affairs." Everyday merchants did not appear to view these administrative controls as an imposition of institutional power, but as local regulation (perhaps what David Singh Grewal would call standards), indicative of "vertical" restriction at the local level, but "horizontal" freedom on a wider scale, with respect to travel and associations with business partners and agents. Despite the role of Andalusi rulers in the governance of trade, Constable asserted that an international trader "was fairly free to trade where, when, whatever, and with whomever he wished."[25]

Network and System Principles and the Gold Trade

The rise of the gold trade in the Islamicate world-system illustrates the changing role of al-Andalus in the network, reflecting many of the precepts of WSA, including the interdependence of political and economic vacillations, and links between fluctuations in traded goods and the prominence or peripheral responsibility of ports, towns, and regions. Glick argues that the interdependence of the economies of the Latin west, the Greco-Roman east, the Islamicate world, and the Far East can be traced through the flows of gold and silver trade in the Middle Ages.[26] The rise of the gold trade also demonstrates the reach of the world-system, the historical connections between European and African regions, as well as western Sūdān's "historically dynamic part" in the Afro-Eurasian *oikumene*.[27] Starting in the third century CE, traders dealt in gold from the Sūdān – a commodity vitally important to the kingdoms of the Maghreb, the Mediterranean world, and western Europe because of regular shortages of bullion before the later introduction of silver from the Americas.[28] One estimate maintains that at the peak of the gold trade more than a ton reached the medieval Mediterranean annually.[29] During the twelfth century al-Andalus began to play a key role in the Mediterranean gold trade as a centre of transmission especially to European markets. Traders and agents transported gold from Awdaghust through Sijilmāsa, Tahert, and Tlemcen to al-Andalus, while from the twelfth century on a more westerly route from Aghmat to Fes was used. Constable acknowledged the Berber middlemen who facilitated the entire gold trade between the Sūdān and North Africa, although she argued that face-to-face transactions between Sudanese and Mediterranean merchants occurred only in the late Middle Ages.[30]

Mediterranean access to gold depended on varying alliances among Berber tribes and North African polities. When the North African Almoravid and Almohad rulers created a vast western empire in the eleventh and twelfth centuries, the flow of gold and trade more generally was stifled to the east, although Andalusi markets and mints assumed greater prominence. The Almoravid gold dinar (*murabiṭūn*) dominated the previous standard currency in the Maghreb, the silver dirham.[31] The Almoravids minted the dinar in the Maghreb from 1068 and began casting it in al-Andalus in 1096 at their capital of Seville. In his *Kitāb al-masālik wa-'l-mamālik* (The Book of Routes and Realms), the Andalusi geographer, theologian, philologist, and botanist al-Bakrī (Abū 'Ubayd 'Abd Allāh b. 'Abd al-'Azīz al-Bakrī) described gold coins in the West African trading town of Tadmekka, south of the Sahara in Mali, just as the Almoravids began minting in the Maghreb in 1068. Al-Bakrī's account reflects precepts of WSA in detailing the fluctuations in traded goods given the rise of the gold trade, as well as the shifting prominent and peripheral roles of towns and regions with the expansion of the Almoravids and the eastern movement of the Fāṭimīds. According to al-Bakrī, of all the towns in the world Tadmekka most resembled Mecca, thus giving it its name, which means "Mecca-like," a reference perhaps not to their spiritual resemblance, but to Tadmekka's likeness as a dynamic site of trade, since it was located at the southern limit of the camel caravan routes that crossed the Sahara. The Berber Tuareg tribe, associated with caravan travel and trade, governed Tadmekka, where they produced gold dinars probably starting in the ninth or tenth century CE. It is likely that they supplied gold to the Fāṭimīds by the tenth century and later to the Almoravids of North Africa and al-Andalus, "whose prestigious coinage was even known in China."[32]

Although Andalusi gold minting started at the beginning of the tenth century with 'Abd al-Raḥmān III, the later *murabiṭūn* gained widespread, unprecedented influence in the Islamicate west, northern Iberia, and southern Europe. Constable argued that the subsequent founding of mints in Almería, Denia, and Valencia in eastern al-Andalus may have been due to increased commercial contact with Italian merchants, and she further attributed the *murabiṭūn*'s popularity to its serendipitous rise at the same time that European rulers became interested in the accumulation of gold. Constable pointed to references to the *murabiṭūn* in Italian documents starting in the mid eleventh century as evidence of a "widespread familiarity" with the coin, although Glick's argument goes even further in asserting the chronic interdependence of the Islamicate world-system and the economy of "the Latin West."[33] The evidence from the history of trade in gold reinforces this interdependence and demonstrates deeply rooted connections between non-modern Europe, North Africa, and the Middle East, as opposed to mutual separation and isolation. This is further evident in the economic activities of the Castilian king Alfonso VIII (ruled 1158–1214), who began minting the *morabetino alfonsino* or *maravedí*, a name derived from *murabiṭūn*, at some point between 1172 and 1174. Northern Iberian kingdoms clearly were familiar with Andalusi gold, since early *maravedís* bore an inscription in Arabic that referred to the Pope as the *imām* or spiritual leader of the Catholics. This political and economic connection between Castile and al-Andalus parallels their cultural link in what Glick calls "the Andalusi cultural polarity," that is, the cluster of habits, practices, and values that emerged from al-Andalus and shaped Iberia's cultural organization for a time.[34] The inscription on the *morbetino alfonsino* indicates one instance in which early minters under the aegis of Alfonso VIII relied on the Andalusi cultural polarity for their cultural and economic models.

This evidence of Arab coinage could be applied to reassessments of transactions between Muslims, Christians, and Jews or to other economic themes in literature, as in the *Cantar de mío Cid*. Since religious and cultural identification was not a barrier to economic interaction between different peoples, the scene with the moneylenders Rachel and Vidas may benefit from re-evaluation. Joseph J. Duggan asserted that the Cid, in seeking to trade the trunks for cash, wanted to avoid the perception that he possessed a trove of Arab coins, which he may have received from the *tā'ifa* king of Seville, al-Mu'tamid (1040–95). Duggan reasoned that the Cid sought to exchange the currency of the Arab economy, gold dinars, for the silver marks with a Christian stamp, presumably because the hero wished to reintegrate himself into Hispanicate society, reconcile with King Alfonso VI, and regain the king's favour.[35] Familiarity with Andalusi products and trade in Hispanicate kingdoms, however, and awareness of the greater stability and prestige of the Arab coin make it difficult to concur with Duggan entirely about the Cid's rejection of gold dinars, especially since the Almoravids began minting *murabiṭūn* in the Maghreb in 1068, thus during Rodrigo Díaz de Vivar's lifetime.

We will see in addition that the importance of the social in Islamicate merchant partnerships further reinforces Duggan's conclusion about how the *Cantar de mío Cid* brings to the fore "in more specific ways than other Western European epics the reciprocal obligations that hold society together." These reciprocal obligations are undoubtedly linked to the work's Iberian, Andalusi milieu with ramifications in the work in gift-giving, the acquisition and distribution of goods, and the economic purpose of the two marriages of the Cid's daughters, Elvira and Sol.[36] The connection between ethical, social norms of conduct and economic praxis in Islamicate trade and the *Cantar de mío Cid* illustrates and highlights their intimate link in pre-industrial exchange, as discussed above in the introduction.

Partnerships and Trade

The Islamicate trade system operated according to standards of reciprocity and trust that are evident in the key role of merchant partnerships. Arrangements between Jews, Muslims, and Christians were central to the Islamicate trade system, characterized by scholars as cooperative and unfettered. However, reassessments of the cooperative view of non-modern trade point to conflicts between traders caused by individual interests and ambitions, along with legal prohibitions in the Islamicate system.[37] There is legal evidence from North Africa and al-Andalus in the writings of Ibn Ḥazm (d. 1064) and Ibn Rushd (d. 1126) that trade was discouraged to non-Muslim regions, although Constable maintained that such dissuasions were often overlooked in the everyday world.[38] Other legal writings from the medieval Islamicate world demonstrate a more tolerant, practical stance toward commercial partnerships and associations, such as the eighth-century books of the Ḥanafī scholars, whose laws were effectively created by merchants and responded to their needs.[39] In medieval Iberia, Jewish merchants dominated many facets of exchange until approximately the mid-twelfth century. Constable argued that Andalusi trade with Hispanicate kingdoms was limited before that time, although Muslim traders were present in northern Iberia and merchants from Hispanicate and European realms trafficked in al-Andalus from the tenth century.[40]

Scholars agree that reciprocity among traders and agents was the basis or standard of the trade system, rather than the endless accumulation of wealth, prestige, and power. Commercial exchange was complex and diverse, and involved numerous types of merchants who played multiple roles, including producers and dealers, retailers and wholesalers, itinerant and stationary merchants, and women brokers.[41] Individual partners acted in many ways as well: "They could receive, send, carry, buy, and sell goods, they could transfer money, and they kept other members of the partnership or commercial firm informed of local prices, conditions, and availability of commodities."[42] Merchants traded in a wide variety of products, including flax, silk, olive oil, spices, materials for dyeing, tanning, and varnishing, metals, books, aromatics and perfumes, jewellery and semi-precious stones, chemicals, foodstuffs, hides and leather, pitch, and "slaves." They hired personnel to work as agents or scribes, although they largely conducted business on the basis of cooperation and partnerships rather than on employment and service.[43] Agreements ranged from the simple to the complex, but most traders participated simultaneously in several partnerships in order to reduce risk.[44] Constable differentiated informal agreements, as between friends found in letters, from formal legal partnerships within large family networks, or between merchants or agents. However, she also mentioned the difficulty of discerning partnerships from the "many instances of cooperation" found in letters, as when a merchant gave a friend business advice.[45]

The trade associations in the Geniza documents demonstrate that partnerships were commonly based on reciprocity, friendship, and trust, as well as on informal and formal legal cooperation.[46] The documents regularly use the Arabic terms *ṣuḥba* (companionship; and a kind of relationship between two merchants), *ṣadāqa* (friendship), and *mu'āmala* (cooperation) when referring to informal agreements, which demonstrate that the partnerships were based on "the human qualities of mutual trust and friendship," and not on "cash benefits or legal guarantees."[47]

Merchant partnerships were not arranged according to the vertical hierarchies often presumed in discussions of medieval economic arrangements, as in feudalism, or in the modern world-system. Vertical, top-down relations were rare in the non-modern system, leading Greif to affirm that partnerships among the Maghribi traders of the Cairo Geniza were organized along a horizontal rather than a vertical trajectory with a communal social arrangement. Greif argues that partnerships between Jewish merchants and their overseas agents reinforced collective rather than individual socio-economic arrangements, which contributed to the development of cooperative merchant practices among Maghribi traders, such as sharing information with other merchants and agents in their group. Neither Maghribi merchants nor agents constituted a dominant or hierarchical class over the other: "Traders did not belong to a 'merchant class' or an 'agent class.'"[48] Rather, traders often served as agents for other merchants, as in the case of sedentary traders who operated as agents for travelling merchants. Greif maintains that collective cultural beliefs among Maghribi merchants affected their business associations, and he argues that merchants and agents formed partnerships based on shared information about people's reputations and past conduct, rather than on impersonal criteria such as profits.[49] He contrasts these horizontal relations to what he views as the vertical partnerships between merchants from other regions, such as wealthy Genoese traders and the poor agents they employed.[50]

Merchants believed that agency agreements were crucial to their business success, and Greif considers such agreements the rule rather than the exception. Agents were hired in foreign ports to provide a variety of services, such as the safe loading and unloading of goods, the identification of potential buyers, and price setting.[51] Few cases of cheating or embezzlement are cited in the documents, which reinforces the basis of the associations in trust. Greif maintains that potential for embezzlement by overseas agents was not managed by legal contracts or other means, or through the hiring of family members as agents. Rather, he points to an information network that established people's reputations, making it mutually beneficial for merchants and agents alike to conduct business honestly.[52]

Merchants could enter into several kinds of formal commercial agreements, all of which were common in medieval Islamicate realms. In the Andalusi milieu, Constable claims that the most common arrangement was the *qirāḍ*, a partnership between one or more investors who provided the capital, and one or more factors who carried out the work. Profits were distributed unequally with the investor receiving a two-thirds allocation because of his financial risks, while the factor was apportioned one third for meeting physical dangers. Similarities between these partnerships among merchant networks of different faiths have led some scholars to conclude that interfaith cooperation at this level was common. For example, it is possible that the medieval European partnership called the *commenda* (from the Latin *accommendatio*), which was first recorded in a Venetian contract in the year 1072, derived from the *qirāḍ*. Constable, however, contended that these analogous contracts, rather than indicating interfaith partnerships, demonstrated "the parallel interests of mercantile business," as well as the exchange of techniques among Christian, Jewish, and Muslim traders.

Partnerships between Andalusi merchants were no different than those in other parts of the Mediterranean.[53] S.D. Goitein and Constable cited one in which two Jewish merchants both named Ibrāhīm b. Mūsā, one of whom was from Mallorca, entered into "a model partnership" or "a basic *shirka*" (a collaboration between investors of capital and those who provided labour in profit-seeking ventures), in which each invested 200 dirhams for travel to an unnamed location. The two merchants would "sell, buy, take and give and do business with their capital and their bodies." Constable observed that partnerships with shared resources like this one reduced risk and increased profits.[54]

The standards of reciprocity and trust did not make partnerships idyllic. In her discussion of merchant misconduct in the Geniza documents, Jessica L. Goldberg argues that traders accused partners and agents in oblique or indirect ways rather than directly confronting the accused, suggesting that more serious allegations were made through the legal system.[55] Many scholars agree that embezzlement and fraud were rare between medieval partners and agents, although cases certainly exist, as evidenced by a tenth-century legal dispute between two partners, one in Qayrawān and the other in al-Andalus.[56] In another example from the Jewish court at Denia in al-Andalus in the year 1083, a man named Isḥāq b. Ibrāhīm accused the servant of another man of keeping the earnings from the sale of cinnabar for himself, instead of handing them over to another partner. The servant, who was never convicted, had been acting as travelling agent for his employer.[57] Despite these problems, reciprocity and trust seemed to predominate as system standards.

System Realignments

Realignments in Mediterranean commerce starting in the thirteenth and fourteenth centuries among Catalan, Genoese, and Muslim realms brought about a series of changes in the Islamicate trade system. Instead of interpreting such changes as absolute and overarching, network theory and WSA indicate that they are better understood as a series of adjustments that occurred over time. Modifications in the system resulted in the development of new trade routes and itineraries, as well as shifts in the production and trade of goods in Iberia, as from silk to wool. Whereas sea merchants who appear in the Geniza documents had followed a southerly route along the coast of North Africa and eventually to Egypt, later traders favoured itineraries that carried them through Mediterranean islands that were newly ruled by European forces, including Mallorca, Menorca, Sicilia, Sardinia, and the coastal isles of Ifrīqiya, which were controlled by the Crown of Aragon in the late thirteenth century. Constable, in examining voyages of the fourteenth and fifteenth centuries, noted triangular configurations that differed from the formerly east-west routes traced along North Africa's coast. For example, in 1464 a Genoese boat sailed from Genoa to Alexandria, Tripoli, Jerba, Tunis, and Málaga. In addition, some vessels only travelled on western Mediterranean routes, such as a Catalan ship in 1327–1328, which stopped in Tunis, Sardinia, Mallorca, Almería, and Málaga, illustrating the gradual change in commercial traffic "through Christian ports."[58]

These changes clearly occurred over time, as evidenced by the diminished role of al-Andalus as a destination for merchant travel between the early and the latter eleventh century. This fact Goldberg attributes not to Andalusi economic shifts, but to the rising instability of the central Mediterranean "as the transfer pivot between the east and west."[59] Realignments in the central Mediterranean resulted in the growth of ports in North Africa and the more frequent presence there of Andalusi ships and thus of Andalusi traders in Egyptian markets. The Geniza letters reveal important changes in merchant perceptions in the late eleventh century, one of which was that traders from Fusṭāṭ no longer perceived Andalusi brokers as partners and associates in their merchant network, despite active trade participation by Andalusi merchants in the Islamicate system.[60]

Iberian rulers and merchants played a key role in the realignment of Mediterranean trade, a shift broadly characterized by the gradual European dominance of routes in the Atlantic and Mediterranean and the development of Muslim-Egyptian trade in the Indian Ocean and the Red Sea. In contrast to the consolidated, Islamicate-dominated trade of earlier periods in the Mediterranean, Iberian port cities in the later Middle Ages were diverse in their interests, trade route connections, and merchant populations. The cities were grouped by Constable into three regions: northern Castile and Portugal, Andalusia and Granada, and the Crown of Aragon. Northern cities controlled traffic in the Bay of Biscay and from northern Europe, and were increasingly involved in trade with England and Flanders. Southern cities such as Seville, Granada, and Málaga largely became way stations for foreign trade, especially between the Atlantic and the Mediterranean, while the Crown of Aragon competed with Genoa and Venice for commercial control in the Mediterranean. European ports during the late Middle Ages enacted diverse policies regarding trade and exacted varying tariffs, in contrast to the consistent regulation of Andalusi ports prior to the period of European expansion.[61]

Due to the fragmented interests of European rulers in the late medieval Mediterranean world, associations between kingdoms began to play a dominant role in commerce, reducing the importance of merchant partnerships in earlier eras and demonstrating shifts in system standards. Government authorities managed and regulated merchants and goods more than during the Islamicate period:

> Overall, Muslim rulers in al-Andalus had been more concerned to profit from international commerce than to restrict it. In contrast, their Christian successors were interested in regulating the movement of merchants and commodities, but generally participated less directly in trade and commercial shipping.[62]

Individual traders experienced more direct governmental controls and pressure than merchants in the earlier Islamicate commercial network.

Perhaps the first signal of the rising importance of associations between kingdoms occurred in 1137–8, when Genoa signed a treaty with the Almohads that opened the way for Genoese trade in Maghribi ports.[63] Hispanicate kingdoms followed suit approximately one century later when they began to form strategic associations with one another, with other European sovereignties, and with Islamicate realms. These associations were not always peaceful and often revealed the rivalries of competing interests, such as the struggle for the control of the Straits of Gibraltar after the defeat of the Almohads in the twelfth century, when four Islamicate kingdoms, the Marinīds, the 'Abd al-Wadīds, the Hafsīds, and the Naṣrīds, along with two Iberian sovereignties, the Castilians and the Aragonese-Catalans, vied for power. This rivalry, according to Ross E. Dunn, had little connection to religion, but was due to the desire for political and economic advancement.[64] Despite the occasional bellicose nature of these conflicts, pacts between kingdoms also reflect mutual agreement, which is perhaps one manifestation of the complicated, often ambivalent *convivencia* (cohabitation) that characterized medieval Iberia more generally. Associations involving the Crown of Aragon include its pact with Castile in 1291 for division of commercial interests in North Africa. Castile recognized Aragon's dealings in the central and eastern Maghreb in exchange for Aragon's acknowledgement of Castile's advantage in Morocco. Aragon also negotiated profitable alliances with Muslim rulers such as the Hafsīds of Ifrīqiya (1229–1574), providing the Aragonese kings annual funding and access to Ifrīqiya's ports, mainly Tunis, where they purchased wool, wax, and leather from North Africa and spices from the Middle East. Additionally, the Aragonese forged agreements with the Ziyānids (western Algeria, 1236–1555), who supplied Aragon with gold from Tlemcen in western Sūdān.[65] Despite the realignment of trade during the later Middle Ages, commercial links between Iberia and North Africa continued, and in fact ports at Tunis, Ceuta, and Tangier prospered. Other significant associations included those between the kingdom of Castile and Genoa, as evidenced by the appointment by Alfonso X of a Genoese officer, Hugo Vento, to lead the Castilian navy in 1264. Genoa dominated trade in Castilian-ruled Andalusia, and negotiated with the Naṣrīds of Granada for the rights to trade with Almería and Málaga, along with permission to export dried fruits.[66]

The late medieval shifts away from alliances among individual merchants toward pacts among kingdoms was due in part to the consolidation of new kinds of polities (as evidenced by the incipient Castilian nation-state), which augmented changes in Iberian trade from approximately the mid-fifteenth century, a result of Spain's increased commercial and political expansion. The case was similar for Portugal, whose economic development produced comparable shifts in trade. Anthony Pagden argues that conquest and armed battle began to typify trade and travel beginning in the mid-fifteenth century, in contrast to medieval commercial dealings. Pagden shows that the trade alliances that linked Iberia and Africa before 1447, the year the Portuguese chronicler Gomes Eanes de Zurara ended his *Crónica de Guiné*, were safer and more profitable than conquest. Zurara claimed that people more commonly exchanged merchandise in their encounters before 1447, rather than resorting to force and arms. Pagden argues that early modern conquest assured participants not only commercial riches, but also glory and social advancement, both of which were, he claims, unattainable in the medieval period.[67]

This change in the relationship between Iberia and Africa, from one defined by merchant transaction to one driven by conquest and bellicosity, epitomizes Iberia's characterization as a series of shifting associations through time. The late fifteenth and sixteenth centuries mark a fluid stage of transformation in many of Iberia's network features, as people and goods travelled and flowed in different directions than before. Technological innovations such as the rise of the printing press had significant social, economic, and political impact, and the incipient forging of the nation-state contributed substantially to changes in sociopolitical arrangements. It is important to note, however, that the years 1492 and 1500 denote neither unqualified shifts in economics, politics, and society, nor utterly transcendent change in the societal ethos and standards, despite the move from merchant partnerships and transactions to political alliances or greater pugnacity between kingdoms. Network theory and WSA offer methods for assessing historical change through attention to continual modifications and adjustments in fluid networks and systems, rather than relying on rigid presumptions of power, hierarchies, and periodization.

Chapter Four

Non-modern Iberian Travel and the Islamicate Travel Network

The Islamicate travel network demonstrates many of the network and system features developed by Manuel Castells and Immanuel Wallerstein, such as links between massive regions in Asia, Europe, and Africa, and the shifting roles of central and peripheral nodes or locales. Network features of vertical and horizontal management and organization are also evident in Islamicate trade, which was a mainstay along the travel routes. As has been noted, political borders did not limit travel or mobility in the travel system, allowing a wide range of traders, teachers, ambassadors, pilgrims, servants, warriors, and poets to move throughout the Mediterranean, northern Europe, Asia, and North Africa without the national affiliations that permit, prohibit, and restrict modern movement. In Islamicate realms, furthermore, discrimination against foreign travellers and merchants was indefensible: "Political boundaries were no hindrance to travel, and discriminatory treatment of foreign travelers or merchants was held to be scandalous."[1] This ideal was not always upheld in reality, as the Geniza documents demonstrate; a European traveller had serious difficulties at the port at Damietta, Egypt, and was only able to free himself from imprisonment through heavy bribes. Such were his worries that on a future journey he requested a letter of safe conduct from a local acquaintance that would demand the traveller's safe treatment by captains and sailors. Letters of safe conduct were common when travellers expected to encounter conflict.[2] Numerous accounts, however, attest to peaceful relations between people of different faiths. For instance, Ibn Jubayr (b. Valencia 1145 – d. 1217) reflected on reciprocity between Muslims and Christians in Damascus, while Ibn Baṭṭūṭa (b. Tangier 1304 – d. Morocco 1368–9) was surprised to find the drawing of an Arab on a church wall in Crimea. In addition, Nāṣir Khusraw (b. Qubādhiyān 1004 – d. Yumgān 1072/1078) recounted peaceful coexistence among Christians, Muslims, and Jews in eleventh-century Jerusalem.[3]

North African caravan routes linked the Sahara, northwest Africa, western Sūdān, and centres of learning such as Qayrawān, which were crucial to the cultural and economic development of al-Andalus, and Europe and the Mediterranean coasts more generally.[4] The Ibādīs in Tunisia and Algeria and the Sufrīs in southern Morocco, two Kharijite sects, were pivotal in the development of the Saharan routes to the Sūdān beginning in the late eighth century, and thus facilitated the creation of the system of roads that connected Europe, Africa, and the Middle East.[5] According to Ralph A. Austen, travel by camel in caravans on these roads endured for more than a thousand years, even to the start of the twentieth century, when European-built railroads provided faster means of travel between the Sūdān and the Atlantic Ocean. Northern desert centres included Sijilmāsa and Wargla, while Timbuktu and Gao were important in the south.[6]

Just as al-Andalus was a commercial hub in the Islamicate world-system, so was it central to broader travel flows. It was a travel destination in its own right, and it was a conduit for passage north and south, as we saw in chapter 3 in the case of the Rādhānites. Starting in the eighth century, Umayyad al-Andalus was part of an intellectual network that included not only Ifrīqiya and Egypt, but also Iraq and Khurasan, a historic region that covered parts of modern Iran, Afghanistan, Turkmenistan, Uzbekistan, and Tajikistan. Despite the political and cultural threat that Umayyad dynastic rule posed to their 'Abbāsid rivals in Baghdad, along with the Umayyads' contempt for 'Abbāsid translation projects in the eighth century, the Umayyads shared a profound interest in classical learning with their rivals. Arabic translations of Greek texts circulated east to west along the travel routes, as demonstrated by an array of works on alchemy, botany, geography, grammar, stories and fables, narratives about Alexander the Great, poetry and literary theory, magic, medicine and pharmacology, veterinary medicine, military treatises, music, optics, and philosophy.[7]

The travel narrative of Lisān al-Dīn Ibn al-Khaṭīb (1313–75) highlights the interconnected quality of the non-modern Islamicate travel and trade system, particularly in the Maghreb. Ibn al-Khaṭīb was born in Loja near the seat of Naṣrīd power in Granada, where he actively participated in political life, though he was also involved at the Marinīd court in Fes. He wrote an encompassing collection of writings on the

Islamicate culture and knowledge of his time, including a monograph on Granada that contained an account by a man called Abū 'Abd Allāh Muḥammad al-Maqqarī from Tlemcen, who visited Granada in 1356. Al-Maqqarī told of conditions along the western part of the trans-Saharan trade route during the middle of the fourteenth century, detailing its development through the digging of wells and the providing of security for the merchants, presumably by local desert inhabitants.[8]

The Non-modern Islamicate System and Motivations for Travel

A variety of aims motivated travel in the non-modern Islamicate system, including diplomacy, as demonstrated by the well-known case of al-Ghazal, a native of Jaén, who in 844 or 845 CE led an embassy from the court of Abd al-Rahmān II at Cordova (ruled 822–52) to Scandinavia and the land of the Vikings.[9] However, four interrelated activities predominated in the system: trade, pilgrimage, travel for intellectual pursuits (*riḥla* or *ṭalab al-'ilm*), and travel for saints' veneration. Trade played a fundamental role as we saw in chapter 3, as did *ḥajj* or pilgrimage to Mecca. Before the eighteenth century, commerce and pilgrimage were linked when Mecca served as a gathering place for merchants and their wares from Europe, Arabia, and the Indies. North African travellers often journeyed in caravans to Cairo, and then continued for an additional thirty-five days, approximately, before reaching Mecca.[10] Numerous accounts attest to pilgrimage journeys made to Mecca by Andalusis. Ibn Jubayr (b. Valencia 1145 – d. 1217), who was a secretary to the Almohad governor of Granada, set out twice for Mecca, making a successful *ḥajj* in 1183–5 but only reaching Alexandria in 1217, where he died before reaching his destination. Since Ibn Jubayr was a man of means, he did not travel by caravan to Cairo, but embarked on a Genoese ship in Ceuta, which took one month to reach its destination in Alexandria.[11] Just as people from northern Iberia and southern Gaul were aware of the trade networks in the Maghreb, so would they have recognized *ḥajj* originating in al-Andalus and the Maghreb to Mecca, especially since Muslim inhabitants of Iberian towns as far north as Zaragoza established connections with the Arab east through those very circuits.[12] This demonstrates Iberia's integration in the Islamicate world even in Hispanicate-dominated territory.

The popularity of *ḥajj* for Andalusis shifted depending on its political role at different times, corresponding to the network and system principle of modification in nodes and standards, and to the interconnectedness of different system domains, including cultural, economic, and political. Political motivations notably encouraged the promotion of *ḥajj* in al-Andalus from the eighth to the eleventh century, when Umayyad rulers used it as a way to dignify themselves and their territory in their rivalry with historically more prestigious centres and rulers in Damascus, Cairo, and ʻAbbāsid Baghdad. Dominique Urvoy illustrates this point with a slightly later example from the Ṣūfī writer, Ibn al-ʻArabī (b. 1165 – d. 1240), who described the "saints from al-Andalus" in his *Risālat Rūḥ al-Quds* not merely to show equivalence in the invention of saints between Andalusis and authorities in the east, but to affirm that Andalusis bettered their eastern rivals.[13] Ian Richard Netton also claims that *ḥajj* in the Umayyad period was motivated by the rivalry between the upstart Andalus in the west and the intellectual and political hubs in the east, indicating that the Andalusis encouraged *ḥajj* as a way to compete with their cultural and political adversaries.[14] Urvoy highlights the particularity of the political conditions during the Umayyad period by demonstrating decreased travel by Andalusis in Ifrīqiya and the east from the close of the Umayyad period at the end of the tenth century to the end of Almohad rule at the beginning of the thirteenth century.[15] The Umayyads thus used pilgrimage as a means to augment their prestige and compete with rival eastern centres, revealing a link between the Andalusi political system and developments and shifts in Islamicate and Andalusi travel patterns.

In addition to economic trade and *ḥajj*, medieval people travelled along Islamicate routes for a third reason, known as *riḥla* or travel to acquire knowledge, and *ṭalab al-ʻilm* or travel to acquire religious knowledge, the two overlapping considerably. Sam I. Gellens argues that the concepts deserve a certain status as "a unifying theme of medieval Islamic history," since they were crucial to the development of Islamicate intellectual and spiritual life. Houari Touati concurs, arguing that knowledge and adventure were closely linked, and that medieval people strongly believed that they could not "inhabit knowledge" without embarking on a trip. María Jesús Viguera Molins underscores the intersection of the three kinds of travel, *riḥla*, *ṭalab al-ʻilm* and *ḥajj*, in asserting that Muslim pilgrimage to Mecca was the main channel of cultural and scientific contact between al-Andalus and the wider Islamicate world.[16] Thomas F. Glick implicitly reinforces the junction of these three travel modes when he observes that "the pilgrimage destination of Mecca determined the places visited" by an Andalusi Muslim on the *riḥla*/*ṭalab al-ʻilm*, such as

Qayrawān, Alexandria, and Cairo, all of which had scholarly communities.[17] This is evident in the travels of the physician 'Abd al-Malik (d. 1078), who took advantage of the pilgrimage to Mecca to study medicine in Qayrawān and Cairo. After returning to al-Andalus, he served as physician to Mujāhid, emir of the *tā'ifa* Denia.[18] The *riḥla* constituted the main component of Muslim Andalusi intellectual life, and several thousand biographies attest to the centrality of *riḥla/ṭalab al-'ilm* for Andalusi scholars.[19] In his study of 246 Muslim scholars from the Ebro Valley, Juan Vernet found that one-quarter had studied in the east.[20] Gellens observes that the *riḥla/ṭalab al-'ilm* was often "family oriented," with sons and occasionally daughters accompanying their fathers, other relatives, or a close friend.[21] This characteristic typifies non-modern travel more generally, which people rarely carried out alone.[22] *Riḥla/ṭalab al-'ilm* and *ḥajj* attest to the broad, cross-regional scale of the Islamicate system.

The fourth chief motivation for travel involves journeys to relic sites and saints' shrines in the Maghreb, which began before the Islamicate period and prior to the Common Era, paralleling similar later itineraries along the Camino de Santiago. North Africa and Palestine were the two traditional sites of saint veneration, well before the Camino's promotion by the European institutions that emerged in the twelfth century.[23] Even before the Islamicate period in North Africa, Christians visited shrines in the Maghreb, which Augustine documented when he recorded cures he saw performed at Hippo, as well as miracles publicized in North Africa.[24] The nature and importance of saint veneration in the Maghreb is evident in a study of Moroccan travel accounts between 1300 and 1800 by Abderrahman El Moudden, whose findings attest to travel patterns that also characterized earlier medieval journeys. El Moudden argued that journeys to the Ḥijāz, the Arabian province that includes Medina and Mecca, were the most important trips that Moroccans could undertake prior to modern times. But before travelling east, Moroccans often embarked on circuitous routes in Morocco to visit some of the more famous saints' shrines. El Moudden asserted that travellers' journeys were rarely direct, but were more often meandering "to enable them to visit most of the sacred spots on their way."[25] Local travel often converged with longer pilgrimages in North Africa, since travel to sacred sites in the east was unthinkable for many people; Sylvia Chiffoleau and Anna Madoeuf argue that such travel was replaced in medieval popular practice by "secondary pilgrimages" ("pèlerinages secondaires") to locales of saints and prophets.[26] Diana Webb concurs with this observation in recognizing the predominance of short-range rather than long-distance travel more generally during the early years of European pilgrimage: "for every pilgrim who made the arduous journey to the Holy Land in these early centuries there must have been many more who frequented shrines closer at hand."[27] This assessment also applies to northern Iberia, where secular and ecclesiastic authorities mandated the cataloguing of miracles to attract travellers to the Camino de Santiago, whose routes competed with sacred sites in France, as well as that at San Salvador de Oviedo.[28]

Travel and Intercultural Exchange

Expanding our scope and assessing Iberian travel beyond the Islamicate travel system provides clear examples of cultural exchange in non-modern Iberian travel networks more broadly. The four travel activities in the Islamicate system were comparable to journeys that would later develop along the Camino, with its intersecting routes between Santiago de Compostela, southern France, Germany, and Italy. Diego Gelmírez, archbishop of Santiago de Compostela from 1100 to 1140, in collaboration with the monastery at Cluny, began to promote Compostela as a destination for seekers of relics, a promotion that coincided with the larger political and economic expansion of Hispanicate kingdoms from the late eleventh century on, in large part due to the development of the Camino de Santiago through trade, building construction, and the rise of churches and shrines. The Camino began to flourish as a corridor with various connected arteries of newly developed towns, such as Logroño, Carrión, and Sahagún, along with the long-established *urbes* of Burgos and León.[29]

Although no formal travel for intellectual pursuits existed in Christianate realms as it did in the *riḥla* and *ṭalab al-'ilm*, the Camino is renowned for its cultural exchange, which according to Francisco Márquez Villanueva extended in two directions: it facilitated Iberia's Europeanization through the spread, for example, of "la cultura latino-eclesiástica de Occidente" (western Latin-ecclesiastic culture); and it hispanized Europe through the extension of contributions (including architectural styles) that spread into southern Gaul.[30] Cultural exchange, which was steady between Andalusi and Hispanicate domains throughout the medieval period, was facilitated more generally in part by Jews and Mozarabs (understood both as Christians living in Muslim domains and as Arabized Christians living in other realms), whose travels demonstrate palpable cultural contact among many Iberian kingdoms.[31] It is not difficult to imagine that Mozarab travellers disseminated knowledge of *ḥajj* to kingdoms in northern Iberia and southern Gaul, given that Andalusi Mozarabs were instrumental in the flow of manuscripts, including codices that reached the kingdom of Oviedo from Christian scriptoria in Andalusi Cordova and Toledo in the early ninth century, and manuscripts that travelled from al-Andalus to Ripoll in Cataluña and to monasteries in towns in La Rioja, such as Albelda, Cardeña, San Millán de la Cogolla, and Silos during the ninth and tenth centuries. Manuscripts also travelled in the other direction, as demonstrated by the Mozarab Eulogius of Cordova, who returned to al-Andalus with books from his travels in the Pyrenees in the ninth century.[32] Mozarabs transferred different kinds of knowledge from Andalusi to Hispanicate spheres, possibly including knowledge of *ḥajj* and other forms of travel. In the same way that the four motivations for travel overlapped along the Islamicate routes, it is possible that they coincided as well in the interactions between the Islamicate and Hispanicate settings. In support of this claim, Cyrille Aillet recently emphasizes the understanding of Mozarab identity through "the portrayal of a situation of interaction" ("le portrait d'une situation d'interaction"), which seems to underscore communication and contact between Muslims and Christians.[33]

The growth of pilgrimage along the Camino coincided with and was crucial to the gradual consolidation and shift in Iberian political and economic power from Andalusi to Hispanicate kingdoms during the twelfth and thirteenth centuries.[34] The Camino's development makes plain the argument by José Luis Barreiro Rivas that pilgrimage generally in the Middle Ages constituted an organizational medium across fragmented political space, suggesting that it was a strategy to create political order and consolidate power, equally evidenced by Muslim pilgrimage to Mecca.[35] Network and system tenets about shifting powerful and weaker nodes are borne out by further examination of interfaith connections in Iberian pilgrimage, while the surrounding political and economic powers were undergoing change.[36]

A second area of intercultural meshing along non-modern travel routes was in lodging and accommodations, which varied according to socio-economic class. Hospitality was a cross-cultural tenet of Judaism, Christianity, and Islam, and people were expected to shelter strangers as a way to extend hospitality to others, including pilgrims and messengers. It was thought that a Christian host, a *hospes* in Latin, should convert a stranger or foreigner, a *hostis*, which also meant an enemy, into a *hospes*, which could signify both a host and a guest.[37] This expectation of Christian charity extended to religious orders, whose monasteries often served as lodging places in Christian regions, as they did along the pilgrimage route to Santiago de Compostela.[38] Hospices also appeared along such popular routes, including the Hospital del Rey in Burgos, founded in 1195 by Alfonso VIII along the road to Santiago de Compostela in order to welcome pilgrims, or the hospices at the two major passes in the Pyrenees on the road to Santiago, Somport and Roncesvalles. Although they were not profit-earning institutions, they sometimes engaged in flagrant rivalries to attract travellers.[39] Inns or hostelries varied in quality and size, yet accommodations were usually modest and inexpensive.[40]

Muslim hospitality derived from the principles of *sharīʿa*, which compelled a community of believers, the *umma*, within the Dār al-Islām to effect high social and moral norms of conduct, regardless of the economic or social status of one's neighbour.[41] These egalitarian standards extended as well to the treatment of Christians and Jews in commerce and other realms.[42] Though these standards were ideal, and in fact were contradicted in al-Andalus by legal writings against trade with Christians and Jews, as discussed in chapter 3, legal exclusions were regularly ignored in medieval commerce, as we have seen.[43] In the non-modern Islamicate world, ideals of hospitality toward Muslims and non-Muslims alike were frequently evident in the network of hostelries and warehouses for the storage of goods known as the *funduq* (plural *fanādiq*) in Arabic or the *fondaco* in Italian. The Arabic name originated in the Greek *pandocheion* and Romance variants subsequently derived from the Arabic, as evidenced by the Castilian *fonda*, which today signifies a modest hostel that provides food and lodging. This medieval institution housed a wide variety of people over nearly two millennia in cities such as Valencia, Naples, Damascus, Barcelona, Tunis, Palermo, and Seville, attesting to Mediterranean economic trade and the constant movement of Mediterranean peoples from late antiquity through the Middle Ages.[44]

In a parallel to the increased or diminished importance of nodes and locales of network theory and WSA, the *funduq* was a malleable Mediterranean institution that changed to meet shifting political and economic demands in different communities. For example, with Arab expansion in the seventh century, the *pandocheion* of the Greco-Roman east fused with the *funduq* that was established from Syria to Iberia in order to house merchants, pilgrims, and rulers alike. Although the

Greek *pandocheion* did not cater to traders' commercial needs, the *funduq* in Islamicate realms increasingly accommodated merchants and traders, while also housing a wide variety of travellers. As western European merchants began to trade with Muslims and Jews in the eleventh and twelfth centuries the *funduq* became the *fondaco,* a place to house foreigners in Muslim markets. Merchants were allowed to practice their faith, drink wine, and follow their customs within the *fondaco*'s walls, although their movements and activities were typically restricted outside them. The enclosure of westerners also allowed for greater Muslim control over taxation and profit. Constable asserted that this arrangement partially explained westerners' widespread involvement in Muslim ports, and the contrasting dearth of Muslim commercial activity in Christian realms. However, with European expansion in the eleventh and twelfth centuries, Christian rulers such as Fernando III and Alfonso X of Castile, Jaume I of Aragon, and leaders in the central and eastern Mediterranean incorporated *alhóndigas* and *fondechs* into their fiscal administrations by adapting them to accommodate the economic needs of their kingdoms.[45] These brief comments show that the non-modern institution of the *funduq* may be examined as a transregional, cross-cultural system within a larger non-modern Islamicate or Iberian travel network.

Chapter Five

Feudalism, "Slavery," and Poverty

Revisions to the historical concepts of feudalism, "slavery," and poverty contribute to the idea of Iberia's non-modern socio-economic organization as a network, rather than as conforming to a set of rigid, circumscribed conditions. The application of system principles as proposed by Manuel Castells and Immanuel Wallerstein, in order to explore the function of power, dependency among nodes, vertical relations and hierarchies, as well as collective versus individual identity, demonstrates that feudalism, "slavery," and poverty were malleable, relational circumstances whose definition changed over time.

Feudalism

Abilio Barbero, Marcelo Vigil, and Thomas F. Glick have examined and debunked traditional expectations about the supposedly unyielding, hierarchical structure of Iberian feudalism, in which landholding nobles ostensibly exercised power vertically over oppressed peasants.[1] Glick adopts the model of the system to compare socio-economic and political conditions in al-Andalus and Hispanicate Iberia, arguing that Andalusi and Christianate leaders maintained political control across time through a continual process of simultaneous stability and change, which he calls crystallization and decrystallization, in the socio-economic arrangements designed to manage and contain the distribution of resources.[2] The development of "feudal relations" in Catalonia and Castile exemplifies these concurrent processes of qualitative continuity and structural change. Given that Al-Andalus and the Islamicate world more generally were not feudal societies, contrasting them to Christianate realms, according to Glick, demonstrates the limits of indiscriminate, universalizing theories of medieval feudalism across cultures. Feudal relations did not develop in al-Andalus because peasantries were not involved in dependent relations with seigniorial nobilities, a consequence of the presence of tribal affinity throughout Andalusi history. Furthermore, lower-class populations were more varied and "less monolithic" than in Christianate Europe, another factor that curbed feudal development in Islamicate society.[3] A final impediment to "feudal" development in the Islamicate world were the prohibitions of *sharīʿa* law, which prior to the rise of new institutions during the sixteenth century, forbade the domination of landholders and political authorities, as well as the accumulation of power by public administrative or corporate entities, preventing the prominence of estates, municipalities, and guilds as in the medieval west.[4]

Glick's comparative study of Castile and Catalonia through the twelfth century demonstrates the expansion of feudal relations across varied cultural, economic, and political spheres, emerging in measure with weak kinship bonds that structured social arrangements. Feudal relations did not develop from individual or corporate rights over land and/or means of production, which Glick explains in agreement with Marc Bloch: "Feudal relationships come into existence only at the expense of kinship arrangements, which they were designed to replace or to compensate for."[5] "Feudalism" was primarily "a system of political organization" that operated according to a set of generalized norms mainly centred on the idea that no one "should be without a lord," rather than on the basis of vertical hierarchies defined by unlimited covetousness. Feudalism's link to economic functions lies not in a traditional focus on ownership of production, since ownership was shared between peasants and nobles, but in the social *organization* of production, a conceptual shift that requires more research into technological and cultural factors.

In order to demonstrate the change to a feudal organization, Glick cites the work of Barbero and Vigil, who contended that feudalism in *aldeas* (villages, large aggregations of people) in Cantabria, the eastern Pyrenees, and Castile and León evolved from kinship groups in dependent relationships with "primitive chiefs." Prior to feudalization, blood relations of group members conferred the right to dispense with collective land settlements or *aprisones* (*presuras* in Castilian), and these were converted into feudal *señoríos* (estates, domains) whose rulers descended from the "primitive chiefs" of the original kinship circle. One clear sign of the transition from kinship to feudal organization was the practice of profiliation, a fictive adoption of individuals and entities outside the kinship group, such as monasteries, which were named in letters that avowed the transfer of land and other possessions. Glick concurred with Barbero and Vigil in noting that letters of profiliation were a mechanism used to erode the authority of consanguinity throughout northern Iberia.[6] Thus, the hierarchies implicit in feudal relations derived from social relations already inherent in complex, progressively weakened kinship relations, and were not due to nobles' hypothetically "natural" proclivity to acquire wealth at the expense of lower-class peasants. Glick observes that seigniorial elites "extracted the surplus produced by the peasants" by what he calls "extraeconomic" means, which refers to the range of non-economic factors that include kinship and "the culture of aristocratic society."[7]

Recent discussions of feudalism invoke the notions of dependence and mutual dependency, which are also crucial in the links between nodes or centres and peripheries in networks and systems. Dependence was not necessarily detrimental and divisive in feudal relations, but emerged as a result of the social organization of production: "Dependence was shaped and constrained by the social organization of production, its technological base, and the political culture, whether of tribal or other inspiration."[8] Glick contends that dependence was based on the socio-economic and political arrangements between groups of people, rather than on land tenure arrangements. There is no doubt that feudal dependence involved vertical relations between peasants and elites, although they developed in complex ways, since peasants shared ownership of production, were pivotal contributors to technological invention, and frequently used legal systems to maintain local control over the means of production, such as water, thus defending against potential takeovers by wealthy elites.[9] These variables suggest that power operated in diverse ways in relations of mutual dependency between upper classes and peasants, and they explain why Glick insists on historiography that addresses feudal dependence as the result of the constraints identified above on the organization, and not on the ownership, of production.

Technology was the most significant constraint in this process, and it is an aspect of feudalism whose importance is underlined in network theory. Glick's argument implicitly highlights the role of culture and cultural values in the "feudal" system, just as Castells insists on the historical contexts and social conditions that conspire at different times to produce networks today, as discussed in chapter 2. Developments and changes in the construction of mills, along with their concomitant relationship to hydraulic systems and irrigation, exemplify technology's pivotal role in feudalism's rise. Glick concurs with Miquel Barceló and other historians, who argued that different mill types, whether vertical or horizontal (a reference to the wheel's placement and direction), "represent different ways of exploiting estates," and thus also different models of socio-economic organization. Horizontal mills were regularly found in tribal societies, as in al-Andalus and other Islamicate realms, which situated them at the end of the canal system designed to divert water for irrigation. Vertical mills were more complex and expensive mechanisms, and thus characterized less egalitarian feudal societies, which placed them at the beginning of the canal system. The mill's location at the end of the system dispensed water equally to tribal members, while its position at the beginning gave precedence to and assured the mill's operation, which from the twelfth century on was largely dominated by the nobility, ahead of peasants' irrigation and labour needs.[10] Glick characterizes these divergent models as the "social ordering of hydraulic space" and highlights technology's role in differentiating the two systems.[11]

Analysing "feudalism" as a system or network raises further questions about collective versus individual identity, particularly when comparing it to the largely tribal organization of Andalusi society. To what degree did the change from kinship to "feudal" systems alter concepts of group identity in Hispanicate realms, and how do they compare or contrast with notions of identity in Andalusi tribal society? Historians argue that Andalusi society retained tribal values and a tribal political organization even after detribalization, when other sociopolitical forms emerged, such as clanic organization and client-patron relations.[12] Glick's comparative discussions of al-Andalus and Hispanicate societies present a variety of contrasting and similar relationships in kinship systems that varied across geographical space and shifted over time. For instance, the kinship systems of Iberia's Hispano-Roman peoples were influenced by the family unit of the Roman *gens*, along with Germanic clanic structure, which until approximately the eleventh century shaped them as largely bilateral and based in the extended family, rather than patrilineal. In contrast, kinship relations of the Cantabri and the Basques, two groups least affected by Roman domination and family patterns, were organized in matrilineal systems.[13]

The well-known figure of Rodrigo Díaz de Vivar (1048–99), the Cid, demonstrates eleventh-century shifts in the Castilian kinship system.

Glick comments on the Cid's *mesnada*, or family kinship group, arguing that the inclusion of family members outside the Cid's bloodlines, such as the husband of his sister-in-law, showed bilateral extension, rather than obligatory genealogical affiliations. The reference to Vivar in his family name, however, demonstrated a change in progress among elite households from bilateral kinship to a foundation in landholding, characteristic of the transition to a more "feudal" socio-economic and political order.[14] Historical analysis and literary representations sometimes converge in discussions of identity and socio-economic or political relations, as in Dolores Oliver Pérez's contention about the resemblance between the *mesnada* of the literary Cid in the *Cantar de mío Cid* and the Arab tribe called the *'aṣabiyya*, which included blood relatives and other supporters.[15] Conversely, Glick suggests an interpretation based on Castilian rather than Arab kinship models, a discrepancy that merits further investigation, especially with regard to the literary and other textual representations of the Cid and his entourage in, for instance, the *Cantar de mío Cid*, the *Estoria de Espanna*, the *Crónica de Castilla*, and the *Versión Sanchina*. Glick addresses cross-cultural similarities of group relations in Cantabrian, Basque, and Andalusi models, but not in Castilian ones.[16]

Tenets of network theory and WSA demonstrate therefore that non-modern Iberian "feudalism" consisted of a complex set of relationships with variability across communities and through time. Glick indicates that the political, social, and economic are intertwined both in the tribal and clanic relations that determined medieval Iberia's social order, and in the feudal arrangements that began to displace them in Hispanicate realms starting in the eleventh and twelfth centuries. This approach to feudalism, with its focus on the organization of resources and production, along with the connections between various social, political, economic, technological, and scientific domains of everyday life, corresponds to Karl Polanyi's claim about the close link between the economic and the social in the non-modern world. It also contrasts with anachronistic assumptions about the primary motivation of non-modern economic activity in the desire for individual gain and profit.

"Slavery"

Network theory and WSA provide frameworks for examining non-modern "slavery" as a multifaceted, transregional system with a polycentric formation comprised of interactive social networks, in which definitions of labour varied culturally and geographically. Recent comments by D. Fairchild Ruggles coincide with this approach in claiming that "slavery was experienced differently by different people, and it was different for men than for women."[17] Scholars have documented many complex types of non-modern servitude, along with a vast nomenclature to describe them from the Middle East to Africa and Europe. S.D. Goitein showed that "slaves" were trusted household members with great independence in ancient Arabia and Israel, as well as in the Mediterranean world, as attested in the documents of the Cairo Geniza.[18] Furthermore, "slavery" is an imprecise translation of a number of words in Arabic, which themselves may have several meanings, such as *khādim*, which generally denotes "servant," but also refers to "black slave woman" in the Maghreb and al-Andalus, and to "eunuch" in the east.[19] Numerous references to *jāriya* (singular) and *ijjān* or *tarājān* (plural) from the Sūdān describe "slave girls" in various ways, including as "virgins," as having one breast, and as good cooks.[20] Merchants in the Geniza documents frequently described male "slaves" as workers in the sectors of trade and finance.[21] Leslie Peirce characterizes "the slave institution" as a customary practice by governing Muslim rulers to consolidate power in their realms. Peirce identifies its inception during the ninth-century 'Abbāsid caliphate, where it was erected for the purpose of creating a "loyal governing class wholly dependent on the sovereign for its status and honors, as opposed to a native nobility whose members might pose limits on the sovereign."[22] This definition clearly diverges from the caricature of the enslaved person as an ill-treated, oppressed laborer, and instead depicts "slavery" as an institutionalized system of state patronage.

Clearly rights of possession of human beings did not wholly define non-modern "slavery," in the same way that ownership of production did not define "feudalism." This is further illustrated by the well-known business partnership between the Indian "slave," Bama, and his "master," the twelfth-century Jewish Tunisian merchant Abraham Ben Yijū. Ben Yijū met Bama while living for nearly two decades on India's southwestern Malabar Coast in Mangalore. The merchant so trusted his Indian colleague that Bama regularly served as Ben Yijū's agent, although they travelled together on other occasions. Geniza documents indicate that Ben Yijū did not travel back and forth between Mangalore, North Africa, and the Middle East, but entrusted Bama with transactions that entailed large amounts of money, even though Bama was probably a chronic drunk.[23]

Non-modern "slavery" was a varied labour system that frequently depended on mutable associations between people, rather than on rigid characteristics of identity or economic coercion. Documents from as early as the ninth century point to Jewish and Muslim merchants who brought Christian "slaves" from northern Iberia and eastern Europe to al-Andalus, and later sent them to differing Islamicate locales.[24] Northern Iberian Hispanicate women were highly valued as entertainers and wives under the Umayyads in al-Andalus, and many such "slaves" produced blond, blue-eyed offspring. In the eleventh-century treatise on love, *Ṭawq al-Ḥamāma* (*The Dove's Neckring*), Ibn Ḥazm claimed that with only one exception the Umayyad caliphs were fair-haired and blue-eyed like their mothers.[25] It is unclear to what degree, if any, these women were held against their will or forced into compulsory labour. Peirce maintains that late fourteenth-century Ottoman sultans "acquired" women concubine consorts in three ways: by capture in battles or raids; by purchasing them on the "slave" market; or by receiving them as gifts. However, in Umayyad al-Andalus, Ruggles argues that if "wives, concubines, and daughters of the Umayyad house" were unable to make their mark by giving birth to a prospective dynastic leader, potentially they could become patrons of "the built environment," along with the literary and visual arts. Several concubines commissioned mosques and other objects,[26] which leads to a series of doubts about their presumed disempowerment and lack of agency. It is difficult to reconstruct the details of these women's incorporation into Umayyad courts, though their experience is an example of how multiple factors combined, including the social and the economic, or kinship and work, to form the basis of non-modern "slavery." In al-Andalus, "slavery" was often a system of patronage that allowed people to escape the conditions of their birth, whether economic or social, such as the non-Muslim women integrated into Umayyad families.[27]

Mutable associations between people and fluid concepts of identity are further evident in the thousands of eastern European "slaves" called *ṣaqāliba*, or Slavic "slaves," at the ninth- and tenth-century Umayyad court. Their identity is doubtful and unclear, as Zidane Zéraoui and Roberto Marín Guzmán attest, claiming that *ṣaqāliba* was a generic term for slaves, and not an ethnic group, while Goitein asserts that *Ṣaqlabī* ("spelled in different ways") denoted any European descended not from the Byzantine or Frankish empires.[28] Several former "slaves" became the rulers or emirs of *ṭā'ifa* kingdoms, such as Denia and Badajoz.[29] This aspect of medieval "slavery," in which former "slaves" ascended to high positions of power and wielded considerable influence, was common in the Mediterranean and Africa, confirmed by Goitein in the Geniza manuscripts and substantiated by Elizabeth Isichei in the case of sub-Saharan "slaves" in North Africa, thus casting immense doubt on the definition of medieval "slavery" as a severe system of bondage.[30] The promotion of "slaves" to influential positions points less to "slavery" as a form of labour and more to its connection to Andalusi patronage.

The *ṣaqāliba* dramatically waned in number after the disintegration of the Caliphate at Cordova in 1031 as many rose to powerful political positions.[31] The relative absence of Slavic "slaves" in Andalusi documents beginning in the eleventh century is due to several possible factors, including the increased Christianization of Slavic territory, as well as the reduced demand for "slaves" in al-Andalus following the collapse of the Umayyad caliphate. In addition, the "slave" trade shifted to the sub-Saharan Sūdān in the eleventh and twelfth centuries with the widespread Almoravid and Almohad rule in the Maghreb and al-Andalus.[32] Similar to the changes seen in the role of al-Andalus in the Islamicate trade system, which shifted as a result of political and economic vicissitudes in the peninsula and in other parts of the network, changes in the documentation of *ṣaqāliba* demonstrate the dependence of "slavery's" definition on variable "extraeconomic" factors, such as Almoravid and Almohad governance.

The notion of "slavery" in a sub-Saharan context included individuals who ranged from a pawn whose servitude ended upon payment of a debt, to a powerful, wealthy court "slave" whose life always depended on a "master" or patron, to wives and women concubines, and people captured through violence. The commonality among them was their lack of lineage, which meant they had no "social identity" in the captor society. Isichei asserts that the conditions and realities of "slaves'" lives were "enormously nuanced, variable and complex." Their daily tasks were no different than those of non-"slaves," although Isichei also maintains they generally worked harder and were poorer. In some periods, "slaves" contributed to agricultural production on the edges of the desert, while black "slave" soldiers were common at other times. Ralph A. Austen estimated that more than six million "slaves" were transported through the African desert from 650 to 1600 CE, which represents only half the number of people exchanged in the early modern Atlantic slave trade in approximately half the time.[33] While there is little doubt that medieval African "servitude" facilitated the development of the nefarious modern transatlantic slave trade, medieval "slavery" was definitely multifaceted with numerous definitions.[34]

William D. Phillips, Jr recently called medieval "slavery" in Iberia a "complex institution" that manifested differently during various historical periods, although with several continuous features through time. In fact, he claimed that "slavery" was persistent throughout medieval Iberia, and indeed contributed to the growth of slavery in the Americas during the sixteenth century. Yet, Phillips does not address how forms of labour so varied and difficult to define, and which we continue to conflate and classify simply as "slavery," could be described as "persistent."[35] It is evident that scholars use "slavery" to describe labour across a wide variety of geographic regions, including Europe, Asia, and Africa, suggesting its role is linked to a shifting, intermeshed network or system with a variety of definitions. The tenets of network theory and WSA, such as vertical and horizontal political, social, and economic orders, the role of power, the variable meaning of all types of labour, and regional interdependence between centres and peripheries, continue to shed light on this important historical field.

Poverty

Network and system tenets illuminate the mutable conditions of non-modern poverty and the poor, who did not denote a delimited group or economic "class" in the early middle ages. Instead, Mark R. Cohen submits that the poor referred to a "political and social category" of the weak, in contrast to more dominant sociopolitical groups. Poor people comprised workers from low economic strata variably identified as peasants, tenant farmers, and rural and town laborers, although it is unknown to what extent they lacked the same resources and resembled one another in their ostensible need. Historians such as Cohen have examined the poor over time in a changing system of destitution, from the early medieval intermeshed sociopolitical category of the weak, to an increasingly identifiable impoverished class starting in the twelfth and thirteenth centuries.[36] The rise of urban communities in Europe, along with the region's growing economic dominance in the twelfth and thirteenth centuries caused the number of poor to increase in Christianate realms. Cohen claims that the growth of an urban, monetary economy probably compounded their numbers beginning in the twelfth century, although Michel Mollatt asserts that their class identification was also likely related to the late medieval appearance of poor people in tax rolls.

Relief for the indigent became more organized and systematic in the sixteenth century, as aid shifted from monastic domains into secular or state hands.[37] Hence, social, economic, and political readjustments all played roles in the changing nature of non-modern poverty and the impoverished, as they did in trade and "slavery."

The practice of charity further demonstrates the variability and connected quality of non-modern destitution, especially in Judaism, as attested by the documents of the Cairo Geniza. Charity was, however, an important concept and activity at different times in Christianity, Judaism, and Islam. Jewish and Christian authorities considered poverty a social ill that demanded redress, a sentiment that Islamic leaders adopted as well.[38] The Geniza documents confirm that the Jewish community at Fusṭāṭ was a nexus of assistance, where even lower class people of humble means contributed to the needs of the indigent.[39] Goitein further maintains that the Jewish community insisted on the education of poor and orphaned children, which may have discouraged child labour.[40] Other experiences of poverty in the Jewish community are readily evident through the Geniza documents, which recount examples of impoverished widows, temporarily indebted merchants, and the chronic poor.[41]

Conversely, taxonomies of the impoverished are more difficult to derive in Andalusi and northern Hispanicate realms. The absence of documentation in Hispanicate Iberia may be due to the decentralization of "urban functions," such as political and judicial administration, the "exchange of goods or information, and the transfer of surpluses from a rural hinterland to a central point." Whereas historians manage to identify these tasks as concentrated in Andalusi towns, they are difficult to isolate in northern Hispanicate kingdoms because the documentation was more dispersed among secular and ecclesiastic courts.[42] In medieval Castile it is generally challenging to identify the poor before the late thirteenth and early fourteenth centuries, since they rarely appear in documents before the 1220s, even in monastic records.[43] Yet in some cases, as in the "free migrants" who settled the Duero Valley region and created a number of settlements and villages during the ninth and tenth centuries, lower class people operated in collectives that managed the sale of land, mills, and water rights, as described above. Glick notes that the ownership of mills in Castile and León differed from typical situations in the rest of Europe, where kings or territorial lords had proprietary rights. Lay lords and ecclesiastical institutions eventually owned the majority of mills in Hispanicate Iberia, although non-noble proprietorship continued, as we have seen. Living conditions for workers changed with the growth of seigniorialization from the eleventh through the thirteenth centuries, which was dominated by ecclesiastical domains but took various forms in northern Hispanicate realms. As indicated above, Iberian seigniorialization reflects a general European trend to limit peasants' freedoms and strengthen their dependence on a lord. Workers involved in *behetría* (*benefactorium*) contracts in Castile and León were free to farm their land, although they paid rent to a lord (*senior*) in exchange for protection. These peasants were not exclusively bound by their agreements, since they could cancel their contract at will and move to different locations. Some seigniorial tenants formed brotherhoods (*hermandades*), which empowered them in ways that individual contracts did not, as evidenced by a *hermandad* in Sahagún that opposed the excesses of the Abbot in 1111.[44] As we have discussed, medieval labour conditions in Iberian territory, especially in "feudalization" until approximately the thirteenth century, were not commensurate with what we would categorize as abusive and systemic impoverishment.

Despite the centralization of urban administrative responsibilities in Andalusi towns, information is scant about poor or working-class Andalusi Muslims. Historical sources contain documentation about the Andalusi urban lower class called the *'amma,* a varied group that included workers, small merchants, and artisans, such as potters, musicians, silk weavers, paper makers, and cotton workers. Furthermore, Andalusi "slaves," a vague, fraught term as discussed above, usually appeared in domestic, military, or administrative settings, rather than agrarian ones.

With regard to *mudéjares,* or Muslims living in Christianate realms, twelfth- and thirteenth-century Latin and vernacular sources from the Ebro Valley and Valencia provide information about the conditions of rural tenant-farming *mudéjares* called *exaricus* in Latin or *sharīk* in Arabic, meaning a partner or party "to a sharecropping tenancy contract." The contractual conditions of this Muslim "contract-tenant" living under Christianate rule were virtually the same as those residing in Islamicate realms, since the individual was bound by an agreement that granted her partial ownership rights and a perpetual lease at a fixed rate. In addition, the worker could transfer at will the rights over property contained in a contract. Glick concludes that this arrangement benefited Muslims living in royal domains, such as those in the Ebro Valley in the thirteenth century, more than their Christian counterparts in seigniorial realms.[45]

The political and economic expansion of northern Hispanicate kingdoms led to the founding of towns that eventually directly affected the classification of the poor. Whereas early towns such as tenth-century León were established as a result of military or political need, urban development in the late tenth and eleventh centuries was due to economic growth, including agricultural production and the subsequent urbanization of Barcelona, the economic stimulus along the pilgrimage route to Santiago de Compostela, and the weakening of political and economic hegemony in al-Andalus.[46] With the increased consolidation of Hispanicate control in the twelfth and thirteenth centuries, authorities began to identify the poor as deserving of charity, promotion, and salvation in late medieval and early modern Castile.[47] This identification coincided with the appearance of poor people in miracle stories, such as Gonzalo de Berceo's *Milagros de Nuestra Señora* and the *Cantigas de Santa María* of Alfonso X, in which the poor sometimes faced grave adversity. After 1300, municipalities in Castile became more active in the care of the poor, supplementing what was previously provided only by monastic orders.[48] This trend toward state aid continued with the growing secular role in caring for the destitute in the sixteenth century as mentioned above.

Conclusions

Feudalism, "slavery," and poverty were intermeshed links of non-modern Iberia's socio-economic network. Studying them from a purely "economic" point of view is profoundly inadequate, since a gamut of political, social, technological, and economic forces converged to mould and shift them at different times. The complex socio-economic organization of non-modern Iberia parallels the variety of economic arrangements in place in North Africa well into the fifteenth century, as attested by literary and legal texts. Traditional approaches that reduced agricultural production, for instance, to a series of contractual agreements are viewed as inadequate by Ramzi Rouighi. He contends instead that an array of different types of taxes, land tenure, and labour contracts coexisted under Almohad and Ḥafṣid rule.[49] Our examination of Islamicate trade in chapter 3, along with the topics addressed here demonstrate similar circumstances in non-modern Iberia, where intertwined socio-economic conditions cannot be summed up by simple definitions of feudalism, "slavery," and poverty, or through the examination of only one region, such as Castile.

Studying these topics as networks or systems reshapes their characterization at specific historical moments, and their assessment and change through time. We have seen that the concepts of poverty and "slavery" became more defined in the late Middle Ages with the economic and political shifts throughout Europe and the Mediterranean. The rise of the Atlantic slave trade, along with the identification of the poor as an economic class coincided roughly with increased European economic power and efforts by European kingdoms to participate in already-existing world-systems that were themselves in decline, as seen in the research of Janet Abu-Lughod. Network theory and WSA are useful tools for assessing change in history, seen here applied to labour shifts throughout the peninsula and the late medieval institutionalization of socio-economic classes, such as the poor. Future applications of network theory and WSA may include focused attention on discrete topics such as specific cities and towns as central and peripheral nodes, along with the development of urban professional elites and their socio-economic impact in fifteenth- and sixteenth-century centres such as Valencia.

PART THREE

New Themes: Politics; Identity and Culture

Chapter Six

Politics

Applying network theory and World-Systems Analysis (WSA) to non-modern Iberian politics and the polity shows not only that discrete domains such as al-Andalus were part of larger world-systems, but also that various Iberian realms operated in a fluid, interdependent political network. We have seen that al-Andalus was politically integrated in the Islamicate world-system and that its participation there contributed to shifts in Andalusi politics, from the period of the Umayyad Caliphate at Cordova to the *ṭā'ifa* kingdoms, to Almohad and Almoravid dynastic rule, and finally to the Naṣrīd kingdom of Granada. The period of political unrest that followed the disintegration of the Caliphate at Cordova in 1031 led to the subsequent creation of Andalusi *ṭā'ifa* kingdoms (from the Arabic *mulūk al-ṭawā'if*) and the expansion of Iberia's northern Hispanicate realms.

Starting in the eleventh century, political associations and power relations between Iberian domains manifest shifts in a malleable, "polycentric formation comprised of interaction networks," as Ray A. Kea suggests.[1] Political realignments starting in the eleventh century between Hispanicate and Andalusi polities cannot be reduced to a simple Christian, Muslim struggle, but rather, reflected larger changes in the Islamicate world-system and in Europe. European economic and political expansion was bolstered by substantial aid in Hispanicate territory by religious groups at Cluny and later Cîteaux. Hispanicate kingdoms were recast to fit European models with, for instance, the change from the Mozarabic to the Roman liturgy, a move facilitated by monks from Cluny.[2] European expansion was one factor in a gradual process of regional political and economic adjustment over many centuries, and was not caused by binary religious antagonism between kingdoms of different faiths. Network and system principles constitute a departure from dualistic thinking that shapes Christian kingdoms and rulers as winners opposed to weak Andalusi losers.

Political adjustment and realignment between different Iberian peoples were constant in history before the eleventh century, as seen in the varying kinds of contact between northern Iberian mountainous tribes and kingdoms, and successive Roman, Visigoth, and Muslim foes. Eduardo Manzano Moreno argues that the northern Iberians who opposed the Muslims in the eighth and ninth century were composed of the same tribes of Vasooni, Cantabri, and Asturi who had battled against the Romans and the Visigoths in previous times. Thus, the Asturian Pelayo (d. 737) challenged Muslim forces not as part of a crusade against Islam, but in defiance of an enemy in the same way that previous generations of Asturians and other tribes had resisted Roman and Visigothic forces. Iberian politics in the eighth and ninth centuries were as complicated as in later generations, demonstrating varied political relations and conflict, rather than absolute, unequivocal conquest. Two Asturian kings, Aurelio (766–74) and Silo (774–83), forged peaceful relations with Andalusi rulers, while a third Asturian king, Alfonso III (866–911), clearly opposed them. The scribe who composed Alfonso's *Crónica de Alfonso III* eagerly discussed predecessors of King Alfonso III who resisted the Andalusis, but failed to examine previous rulers who had diplomatic relations with them, such as Aurelio and Silo, thus demonstrating politically biased historiography, rather than the full scope of past political relations.[3]

Beginning in the eleventh century, *ṭā'ifa* and Hispanicate rulers entered into diverse alliances and struggles for power, as when al-Qādir of Toledo could not protect his domains against impending threats from other *ṭā'ifa* leaders, such as al-Muqtadir of Zaragoza. Instead of appealing to other *ṭā'ifa* kings for aid, al-Qādir called on the Hispanicate ruler of Castile, Alfonso VI. Similarly, al-Muqtadir of Zaragoza asked for assistance from the Hispanicate king of Aragon, Sancho Ramírez, who complied with attacks on Cuenca, which was ruled by al-Qādir.[4] After al-Qādir's capitulation of Toledo in 1085 to the Castilian king Alfonso VI, the remaining Andalusi leaders appealed for help to the Almoravid leader in Morocco, Yūsuf Ibn Tāshfīn. Tāshfīn's forces would eventually link al-Andalus and Morocco in an empire that spanned the Straits of Gibraltar, thus connecting Seville and Marrakech, the Almoravid seat of power. The alliances between Muslim and Christian leaders, such as al-Qādir of Toledo and Alfonso VI of Castile demonstrate that medieval struggles did not always derive from religious difference, as illustrated by al-Qādir's appeal to Alfonso VI for aid, who clearly did not perceive the Hispanicate king as his Christian "rival." Castile's encroachment into Andalusi territory was in fact only one among a gamut of problems stemming from North Africa,[5] which suggests political rather than religious motivations for antagonism and interfaith alliances. Complex agreements were also apparent during the twelfth and thirteenth centuries, when the Almoravids and Almohads vied for power in the Maghreb and al-Andalus. The Almoravids in Iberia appealed to Christian neighbours in the Hispanicate kingdoms of Portugal, Castile, and Aragon for aid in order to avoid succumbing to competing Almohads.[6]

Several examples from the twelfth and thirteenth centuries contrast the conventional idea of Christian/Islamic rivalry and show that Hispanicate sovereigns routinely viewed other Hispanicate kingdoms and Christian dioceses as greater threats to their power than Muslim rulers.[7] Challenges between Hispanicate kingdoms abound, as in the case of Alfonso I, "El Batallador," king of Aragon and Navarre (1104–34), whose final will and testament not only reflected concerns about the Almoravid menace, but also about Castile's potential future dominance and fractures between Aragon and Navarre.[8] Furthermore, the scribes who wrote the *Historia Compostelana*, a twelfth-century chronicle from Santiago de Compostela, deemed the conflicts between Castile-León and Aragon more profound and deleterious than those between Hispanicate and Andalusi kingdoms.[9]

Political readjustments were rampant even in the thirteenth century, which for some scholars represents the decisive, penultimate phase in the dissolution of Andalusi political power before the final capitulation of the Naṣrīd kingdom of Granada to the Catholic Kings in 1492. The rule of King Alfonso X from 1253 to 1284 is emblematic, since his political goals mainly consisted of administrative and political centralization, rather than comprehensive initiatives to diminish or eliminate Islamicate power.[10] Even if the idea of "national" unity existed in fledgling form, Anthony Pym notes that it "disintegrated into a series of internal struggles during and following Alfonso's reign."[11] Furthermore, Alfonso's wish to extend Castile's renown within the peninsula and throughout Europe[12] did not constitute a marauding, crusading military enterprise against Islam. Pope Clement IV, during his rule in 1265, expressed concern about "the reluctance of Christian kings [in Iberia] to eliminate" non-Christians from their midst; Alfonso's dealings with

Granada's Naṣrīd king as one of his vassals exemplified continued associations and realignments with Islamicate kingdoms in Iberia.[13] The king's centralizing goals also represented a novel, large-scale political and cultural project, carried out in collaboration with the largest and most erudite group of Christian, Jewish, and Muslim intellectuals of his time in all of western Europe.[14] Alfonso X's idea of *Espanna* was not limited to Christianate realms, but also included the peninsula's Islamicate kingdom.

Finally, network and system tenets serve to temper the overstated emphasis by some historians on force and military battle as central factors in non-modern sociopolitical change. For instance, Jaime I of Aragon (James the Conqueror, ruled Valencia 1239–76) did not institute Christian-Aragonese rule in thirteenth-century Valencia through force or obligatory conversion of the city's Muslim population; rather, he inherited a pattern of acculturation, common in the Mediterranean and with analogies in Islamicate and Byzantine lands, which consisted of *mudéjares*, the city's Muslim community, leading parallel lives to Christians and Jews. *Mudéjares* did not immediately flee Christian rule, although *mudéjar* elites "progressively drifted toward Granada and Tunis" as the rich, artists, and intellectuals among them grew increasingly dissatisfied with the new Aragonese administration. Although Valencia definitely lost its Muslim leadership over time, Robert I. Burns claims that "the myth" of their mass expulsion cannot be sustained under close scrutiny, since *mudéjar* migration from Valencia was gradual and unsystematic.[15]

There is no doubt that military force was important at times in non-modern Iberia, as in the Visigothic control of the peninsula by armed interventions in Roman military and operational networks.[16] However, network and system principles demand the inclusion of diverse factors beyond military battles, in order to achieve a more nuanced historical analysis. For instance, it is well known that Arabs did not attain political control of the peninsula through battles and the mass immigration of Muslims or Arabs to Iberia from the Middle East and North Africa. Instead, they relied on political centralization, the integration of comparatively few Arabs in the Iberian population, and the eventual conversion of Iberians to Islam.[17]

The Idea of the Polity

Network and system tenets may be applied to the non-modern polity, which we have seen is best construed as a political core surrounded by a sphere of influence, rather than as a rigidly bordered realm. Ralph

W. Brauer argues that non-modern boundaries were not constituted by "a sharp transition from one political entity to the next, but rather a gradual interpenetration of the adjoining communities."[18] Albert Habib Hourani echoed this view in his theory of political arrangements in the non-modern Arab world:

> Before the modern age frontiers were not clearly or precisely delimited, and it would be best to think of the power of a dynasty not as operating uniformly within a fixed and generally recognized area, but rather as radiating from a number of urban centers with a force which tended to grow weaker with distance and with the existence of natural or human obstacles.[19]

Political Islamicate realms were arranged as spheres of influence that radiated out from core urban centres, with weakened capacity the greater the distance from the hub. This is in accord with the role of cities rather than nations or states as the focal point of Muslims' public lives within the larger, more conceptual Dār al-Islām (the Domain of Islam).[20] Legal discourse did not dictate territorial boundaries, since *sharī'a* law was not territorial in nature, but instead centred on individuals' social and behavioural roles.[21] This idea of the medieval polity and its boundaries characterized non-modern Iberian political domains until approximately the thirteenth century and is wholly consistent with variable relations of power in networks and systems, along with the roles of stronger and weaker nodes.

Hispanicate kings did not rule over fixed territory or "permanent human groups," but over places and people whose delimited contours were not always necessary or important.[22] Iberian political rule was not determined by territorial boundaries, but by dominance over variable space whose borders shifted in concert with changing kinship alliances.[23] Thomas F. Glick notes that both Andalusi and Hispanicate kingdoms tended toward uniting and separating, as in the case of Sancho el Mayor (c. 990–1035), who divided his kingdom in three parts, Navarre, Castile, and Aragon, among his three sons, as did Fernando I of León (c. 1016–65). *Ṭā'ifa* kingdoms were no different, exhibiting similar shifts in boundaries due to "family-based mergers and disaggregations," as in the incorporation of Denia by al-Muqtadir of Zaragoza in 1076, and of Lleida-Tortosa, ruled by al-Muqtadir's brother, al-Muẓaffar, three years later.[24]

The role of kinship alliances in forging networked political influence is evident in Pamplona, which eventually became the seat of the kingdom of Navarra. Pamplona was a newly constituted space of power in the eighth century that was difficult to locate with any certainty within "Christian territory," due to the unknown role of Christians there. Two families, the Aristas and the Jimenos, began to consolidate Pamplona's political role in the ninth century, often through family alliances in Hispanicate realms and with dynasties in al-Andalus. Manzano Moreno notes that the tenth-century sovereigns of the kingdom of Navarra rooted their authority in their allegiance to Visigothic legal codes, and above all in their connections in the "complex political mosaic of their time," which included al-Andalus. Hence, Visigothic law and family dynastic ties in Andalusi and Hispanicate realms networked, overlapped, and combined to produce sovereign authority in Navarra.[25] This intermeshed quality demonstrates network and system principles both internally to the kingdom as constructed by webbed family associations, and externally in its relations with kingdoms (families and dynasties) outside its domain.

The forging of the non-modern polity and its political authority through diverse, interacting sociopolitical domains, including kinship and law, parallels Castells's idea of the emerging network state, which we defined in chapter 2 as an emerging political unit composed of intersecting entities such as states and international networks. Despite the anachronistic reference to interacting modern networks, Castells's model helps to rethink Iberian kingdoms not through standards of Christian, Muslim, Islamicate, or Hispanicate purity, but as political entities that gained authority through the activities of overlapping macro- (transregional) and micro-level (local) groups and entities, such as tribes, clans, dynasties, families, legal schools, religious and spiritual communities, and cultural and literary artists and producers. Castells emphasizes an idea of the state as always in process, wholly characteristic of the regular operations of networks and systems, rather than conceiving of the state as a final stage of delimited completion. Pamplona and Navarra exhibited this quality of being in process, where social forces and groups interacted to produce political shifts, with individuals and families weakening over time and others gaining prominence and influence. A similar political pattern dominated in al-Andalus, where changing family alliances also brought about territorial shifts. Political continuity depended on the stability and permanence of the juridical system during the Umayyad and *ṭā'ifa* periods, and on the Visigothic legal codes in Navarra.[26] Glick observed that there was a "convergence in political form, if not in content," in the organization of Andalusi and

Hispanicate cultures, suggesting resemblance between them, rather than absolute division and separation.[27]

Realignments in Political Domains

The application of network and system principles to historical change in the concept of the polity or state requires placement of the concept in always-shifting networks over a long period of time. This avoids the teleological inevitability and triumphalism apparent in traditional historiography on the transition from medieval kingdoms or polities to the so-called nation-state of the Catholic Kings. The interconnected system of political, economic, and social realignments that took place in the twelfth and thirteenth centuries between Islamicate and Hispanicate kingdoms preceded those later developments, and coincided roughly with shifting conceptions of sovereignty and measurable territorial boundaries that contributed to the consolidation of a smaller number of Iberian polities in the fourteenth and fifteenth centuries. Castells's model of the emerging network state also serves to highlight during this later period the meshing of multiple forces in the strengthening of Castile and Aragon. John Watts proposes a networked model in his focus on the overlapping interaction of what he calls multilayered structures, such as law, the courts, lordship, friendship, and professional help in legal matters in the shaping of fourteenth- and fifteenth-century European polities. Watts's approach dovetails with Castells's ideas about interaction, both of which are in accord with Glick's and Miquel Barceló's interdisciplinary hypotheses of connection in Iberia's socio-economic organization, as discussed in chapter 5.[28] Watts critiques biased historiography that identified social and economic decline, along with war and disorder as the causes of state formation in the fourteenth and fifteenth centuries.[29] Instead, Watts maintains, polities took shape as a result of structures that were incomplete, overlapping, and subject to modification. He calls them networks of interaction that can reveal and explain sociopolitical change.[30]

Shifts in the Iberian political system were due not only to external pressures and influence, as from Cluny, Cîteaux, and North Africa, but were also intimately connected to social modifications in local kinship networks (as we saw in our discussion of feudalism in chapter 5), where feudal elites derived from and replaced tribal leaders in kinship groups. These changes further affected economic arrangements, also examined above. Glick concurs with Reyna Pastor in maintaining that the development of Christianate kingdoms and the forging of cultural groups linked to particular geographic areas were carried out by clusters of nobles, who began to observe and identify what Glick calls "ethnic solidarity" among bands of people. Changes in the makeup of these elites, therefore, were crucial in the political rise of Hispanicate kingdoms, in socio-economic developments, and in contributing to broad realignments in Iberian and transregional networks.[31]

Another pivotal shift from the thirteenth century onward was the gradual conversion of the porous medieval border or frontier into the idea of a delimited territorial and political boundary. Emilio Mitre Fernández calls the Iberian peninsula a perfect "laboratory" for tracing the conversion of the frontier into an eventual national boundary, and identifies three factors that initiated the shift in the twelfth through the fourteenth centuries: territorial modifications between Hispanicate kingdoms; the growing awareness of an internal political dimension; and adjustments in the meanings of certain terms, such as *patria* and *nación*, all of which culminated in the late fifteenth-century nation-state of Fernando and Isabel.[32] This convincing equation, however, lacks a material element that definitely overlapped with even if it did not directly prompt some of these changes: the idea of measurable territorial boundaries, which Teófilo F. Ruiz contends was essential to the development of the idea of sovereignty.[33] The interest in spatial delimitations pre-dated what Mitre Fernández identifies as the strengthening of "national" sentiment among the sparring Iberian kingdoms of the fourteenth and fifteenth centuries.[34] Ruiz focuses on changes in the possession of property at the local level, found in his analysis of Castilian wills, inquests, land transactions, and surveys. From the late twelfth to the fourteenth century, these sources illustrate the following:

> Throughout northern Castile, village communities, monasteries, and small landholders engaged in costly litigation, sometimes undertook violent action, and appealed repeatedly to the king for inquests to determine not the extent of their jurisdiction, but the actual spatial extent of their property or communal holdings.[35]

This spatial shift from jurisdictions to quantifiable, measured areas was often carried out through the building, establishment, and identification of paths, rivers, hedges, stone fences, guards, and artificial boundary markers called *mojones* or *moiones*, which local officials, administrators, and land surveyors physically mapped out on foot.

Such efforts accelerated in the early thirteenth century, manifesting in the visible borders of livestock routes of the Mesta (organization of sheepherders) or *cañadas* (extended pastures) that connected northern Castile to grazing areas in Andalusia and Extremadura.[36] Glick argues that herding was so important in the early Hispanicate kingdoms (as it was in al-Andalus, whose political sway was in decline) that the conflicts of "herding peoples" typified frontier relations at that time. Those disputes occurred not only between Berber tribesmen and Christianate herders, but also between different Hispanicate polities, as between Castile and Aragon over the pastures of Soria in the early twelfth century.[37] Hence, shifts in the concept of the border permeated social, economic, and political relations throughout the Iberian network.

Ruiz identified two discourses in the documents he studied, the first centred on jurisdiction, lordship, and the land initiated by powerful secular and ecclesiastical lords, while the second focused on the land's material realities, such as its physical boundaries, and was linked to transactions of common people and rural communities. These discourses demonstrate a tension between the consolidation of estates by nobles and urban oligarchs, and the fragmentation of rural property among peasants through inheritances, a conflict that Ruiz calls "the crux of Castile's rural history."[38] By the fourteenth century this clash contributed to the emergence of oligarchic elites in towns, as well as to the economic divisions among wealthy, rural farmers and disadvantaged peasants.[39] Ruiz's research demonstrates "an explosion" of documents in the thirteenth and fourteenth centuries that became instruments of the wealthy and powerful, such as the Crown, municipal councils, monasteries, and cathedral chapters. These documents include inventories, *repartimientos* (distributions), *apeos* (surveyor's plans), and account books that underscore the sociopolitical divisions of the time through the cataloguing of material goods, as well as property that was spatially measured. Ruiz observes that these taxonomies evidence a very different reality from "the vague formulations of an earlier age."[40] However, they are also features of transregional and local network shifts, and are not the inevitable colonial manifestations of an ostensibly superior, conquering, Catholic-European sociopolitical and economic order.

The local concern with spatial boundaries coincided with a growing royal interest in territorial borders for economic gain and political preservation, as evidenced by the construction of custom houses and toll stations, starting mainly in the thirteenth century. María Asenjo González demonstrates that Alfonso X benefited from the profitability of the border when he instituted a ten per cent tax on merchandise (*diezmos aduaneros*) at toll stations (*portazgos locales*) on land.[41] In addition, he used the network of ports in his realm to collect such payments from ships' cargo.[42] Such financial benefit increasingly characterized border crossings and transactions in late medieval Iberia, while foreshadowing eventual struggles for monetary gain and control in the fourteenth and fifteenth centuries between local interests (lordships, urban oligarchies, and other officials) and the monarchy, as demonstrated by business transactions at Castile's border with Aragon and Navarra.[43] Miguel Ángel Ladero Quesada suggests that the emergence of a system of custom houses and tolls in the 1250s and 1260s constituted a new and unprecedented concept of the border.[44]

The changes in the idea of the border, along with reassessments of political concepts such as the definition of sovereignty and the role of the monarch, coalesced in the fifteenth century with the initial forging of the nation-state by the Crowns of Castile and Aragon, a process that Ruiz explains in the following way:

> I am not arguing that the territorial monarchy in Castile emerged exclusively from a new awareness of the measurableness of the land. The genesis of the idea of sovereignty also resulted from a complex set of circumstances and the slow theoretical elaboration and transformation of the concept of sovereignty itself. Beginning in the twelfth century, a succession of civil and canon lawyers, political philosophers, and other scholars began to enunciate political principles that would, by the sixteenth century, come to be identified with the indivisible power of kings and/or people.[45]

These late medieval developments, which included local interest in the spatial measurement of the land, a preoccupation with inventories, and the establishment of a system of custom houses, were connected to the early, inchoate stages of Spain's national construction. Isabel Montes Romero-Camacho observes that the delimiting of borders by the Catholic Kings had as a consequence the definition and application of a commercial policy, as well as the establishment of custom houses in Castile, which favoured the royal coffers ("tuvo consecuencia la fijación de aduanas en Castilla, lo que favoreció a la hacienda regia" y "la definición y aplicación … de toda una política comercial").[46] The

Catholic Kings reinforced this commercial policy and the political unification of the fledgling state when they eliminated internal custom houses at land entry points called *puertos secos* between Castile, Aragon, and Navarra, transferring them instead to the limits with France and Portugal. José Antonio Maravall interprets this shift in two ways, first as a move toward internal homogeneity (initiated by the development of an internal political awareness in the twelfth through the fourteenth centuries, as theorized by Mitre Fernández), and second, as the establishment of an encircling outward belt that marked the borderline "like a guard adjacent to foreign kingdoms" ("como una 'guarda' frente a los reinos extraños").[47] Yet in the sixteenth century this girdle of custom houses also constituted a heterogeneous rather than homogenous network because of the competing interests of royal, ecclesiastic, feudal, and municipal authorities.[48] Clearly the early modern border was not absolute, since various rival powers such as these vied for its maintenance and control. The early modern border was not a firmly established line that marked the periphery of a newly sovereign Castilian nation; rather, late medieval and early modern shifts constituted the beginning steps in that direction. The custom houses that readers today might expect to be evidence of medieval border crossings are in fact manifestations of the late medieval and early modern effort toward political hegemony and economic reinforcement.[49] We have come a long way from earlier spheres of influence. Medieval references to the border or frontier as a limit to guard and protect were rare indeed. Analysing these later developments as long-term modifications in political networks removes the burden of their justification as they relate to particular dates or date ranges, whether 1492, 1500, or "the late fifteenth century." The principles of network theory and WSA demonstrate that historical change in politics and the polity never occurs in isolation, but always in association with elements in multiple systems or networks.

Chapter Seven

Identity and Culture

Network theory and World-Systems Analysis (WSA) necessitate the adoption of different scopes to examine non-modern Iberian individual and collective identities in diverse networks, such as Iberian, Islamicate, or Andalusi systems. The Islamicate system is macro-scale with a broad extension, embracing the Islamicate trade and travel systems, while the Iberian and Andalusi networks are both micro and macro, since each may refer only to the micro-scale idea of Iberia or al-Andalus, or to a broader, macro-scale concept, including territory in Europe and the Maghreb. The Iberian network would contain nodes identified as, for instance, Asturian, Castilian, Aragonese, Mozarab, *mudéjar*, *converso*, and *morisco*, which would be highlighted through their contrasts and comparisons. Network theory and WSA require analysis of the relations and intersections between those terms, avoiding a narrow concentration on modern terminologies and limits, such as ethnicity, religion, and national affiliation. These methods provide a framework for examining each group not only through their differences, but also as varied, interconnected facets of the Iberian identity system.

The application of the tenets of network theory and WSA requires the interpretation of Iberia's history of identity as a series of fluid adjustments and realignments among groups of people across time, such as Mozarabs, Castilians, *mudéjares*, *conversos*, and *moriscos*, which result in part from changes in other overlapping systems, including the political and socio-economic orders. Use of these methods involves recognizing and deciphering the identity system's standards, along with the modifications that occur as networks shift. This long temporal scope compels an understanding of historical change through realignments and varying standards, rather than as a series of static periods and anomalous events. For instance, the recognition of non-modern identity networks would convert North African immigration to Spain in the 1990s and 2000s from an ostensibly atypical invasion of cultural others, to a modern realignment of historical, political, socio-economic, and cultural networks.

The historical and fictional accounts of Rodrigo Díaz de Vivar (c. 1043–99) illustrate this network application in two main ways. The *Cantar de mío Cid* differentiates two Muslim populations in the Andalusi Muslims called *moros de paz* or "Moors of peace," and fundamentalist Almoravids and Almohads from North Africa. While the *moros de paz* lived as neighbours to Christians in Iberia, Almoravids assailed the peninsula in 1093, while Almohads attacked in 1146. According to Alberto Montaner Frutos, this contrast explains the "attitude of tolerance that is reflected in this poem" toward Muslims such as Avengalvón.[1] Understanding *moros de paz* and North African Muslims as nodes in Iberia's identity system demands their examination as simultaneously similar and different in association with one another, and in relation to other groups represented in the poem. Applying network and system principles to the Andalusis and North Africans demonstrates differing relations of power between the two groups, as well as in relation to two other alliances, the Cid's *mesnada* and the *bando* of the Infantes de Carrión, the Beni Gómez.[2] Including them all in the same identity system undermines presumed hierarchies and affiliations according to "religious" or "ethnic" similarities and differences, since the Hispanicate, "Christian" Infantes turn out to be the Cid's enemies, while the *moro de paz* Avengalvón is his trusted friend.

In addition, the *Cantar de mío Cid* is based on the life of the bicultural, Arabic-speaking historical figure, Díaz de Vivar, who fought in support of the Muslim rulers of Zaragoza against Christians and other Muslims: "Speaking Arabic, living as an Arab, he moved easily between the two societies."[3] Interpreting Díaz de Vivar's cultural fluidity within the Iberian identity system not only reinforces his subjectivity through cultural identification and associations; it also converts his ostensibly bicultural uniqueness into a more conventional way of being in medieval Iberia. Díaz de Vivar lived between two societies, just like many other non-modern Iberians, including Alfonso X (ruled 1252–84) and Ramon Llull (Mallorca 1232–1315). Thomas F. Glick noted that "points of contact" between Christian and Muslim elites made the cultures familiar to one another, thus casting the sojourns of Alfonso VI (1047–1109) in Toledo, his brother García de Galicia (1042–90) in Seville, and the Cid in

Zaragoza (served al-Muqtadir and al-Mutamān, 1081–6) as "typical."[4] Framing the identities of these figures in larger networks would reinforce their characterization as ordinary and customary, and would shift traditional interpretations of non-modern culture and history away from binary separations of Christians and Muslims, or East and West.

Applying network theory and WSA to the study of identity shifts conventional understandings of the group characterizations of Mozarabs, *conversos*, and *moriscos* as homogeneous and absolute. This application confirms revisions of "Mozarab," as discussed in chapter 4, and bolsters Cyrille Aillet's updated meaning through "the portrayal of a situation of interaction," rather than as the result of essential qualities.[5] Studying "Mozarabs" in Iberia's identity network emphasizes their identity construction through communication and contact between Muslims and Christians, rather than through their presumed allegiance to Christianity and Christian people.

The inclusion of *conversos* and *moriscos* in the system opens the scope of analysis to include the fifteenth through the early seventeenth-centuries, thus removing periodization's predictable constraint. This broad perspective shifts the normal interpretation of history away from temporal periods, fractures, or breaks, as in the depiction of the year 1492 as a significant historical divide. It also avoids the use of ontological absolutes, preventing the impression that the forced expulsions and conversions of Jews and Muslims generated circumscribed, inherent identities without a past or future. Instead, the inclusion of *conversos* and *moriscos* as network nodes places them in relation to other node-communities and makes them part of the interplay of the varied power relations involved in the system. This approach also demonstrates simultaneous continuity and change in the cultural standards at work in their construction.

Diminished Reliance on Modern Terms

The application of network theory and WSA reduces the problems in using modern criteria and labels to characterize historical figures along "ethnic" or geographic lines as Arab, African, or European, such as the travellers Ibn Jubayr (b. 1145) and Ibn Baṭṭūṭa (1304–c. 1377). Ibn Baṭṭūṭa would be considered "African" today because he was born in Tangier, but he was of course culturally "Arab." Similarly, Ibn Jubayr was a native of Balansīya in al-Andalus, now Valencia, Spain, which by today's standards makes him "European," although he was also culturally "Arab" and/or Andalusi.[6] It is doubtful that Ibn Jubayr, Ibn Baṭṭūṭa, Rodrigo Díaz de Vivar, and their contemporaries perceived themselves according to these modern criteria. Our examination of the varied significance of tribal associations before approximately the twelfth century in al-Andalus and Hispanicate domains reinforces this doubt, especially with regard to socio-economic arrangements and cultural affiliations. Early medieval collective identities were forged according to affiliations with families and dynasties, with several paradigms indicating fluid modes of identification, such as the Arab *nisba* or "noun of relation," which made identities malleable and shifting. If a name was inherited the *nisba* signalled an individual's connection to a group, such as a tribe, clan, or dynasty, as in *al-Kindī* "of the tribe of Kinda." Conversely, if a name was acquired the *nisba* referred to significant experiences and activities in a person's life, such as important colleagues, teachers, or friends with whom one had created bonds, memorable events, or places of residence, as in *al-Andalusī* "from the Andalus."[7] The *nisba* allowed individuals to establish kinship independently of blood relations, as in the case of the Mamlūk "slaves," who lacked demonstrated lineage and possessed only an *ism* or first name until their rise to power in Egypt in the thirteenth century.[8] Berber families who arrived on the peninsula in the early years of Iberian settlement retained their Berber tribal name, but also adopted Arab *nisbas* due to their genealogical prestige.[9] In chapter 5 we discussed this type of variable identification in Rodrigo Díaz de Vivar's *mesnada*, a bilateral kinship group that included blood relatives and extended family members affiliated by marriage.[10] In the *Cantar de mío Cid*, Michael Harney claims that the Cid's *mesnada* referred not only to the Cid's inner circle, but also broadly and collectively to his large number of followers. Harney contends that the Cid moved between and within communities using diverse understandings of kinship in order to manage conflict and fashion his identity as a father, husband, and leader.[11] Hence, identity in the *Cantar de mío Cid* may be examined from two perspectives of broad group kinship and the Cid's contained self-fashioning, illustrating the multilayered macro and micro scales of analysis that networks and systems permit.

Applying network and system principles to non-modern Iberian identity shifts our reliance away from religion, ethnicity, and "national" affiliation as identifiable features of delimited groups. Thinking broadly about terms such as "Iberians" as diverse, rather than as narrowly circumscribed, encourages us to reconsider categories often taken for granted. "Iberians" had multiple meanings, since at times the term designated the inhabitants of the peninsula's Mediterranean coast, along with Murcia, while on other occasions it comprised the peoples of Andalusia.[12] Because of these numerous referents, historians today such as Fernando García de Cortázar and José Manuel González Vesga do not necessarily understand the Iberians as a delimited ethnic group, but recognize them as a combination of various peoples in diverse peninsular regions, which comprise the Levant, the Ebro valley region, Andalusia, and Catalonia.[13] "Iberians" rarely denoted a category of modern-style identity and social order reflecting nations, ethnicities, or religious attachments. Instead, the term signified a network of variably interconnected and autonomous groups located in a range of Iberian locations.

Just as the term "Iberians" contains variable referents and meanings, so does "religion" function in multiple ways in the Iberian identity system, signifying antagonistic conflict at times and quiescent stability at others. Olivia Remie Constable made the arguable claim that religion constituted the main point of difference in personal identification in the Middle Ages, while María Rosa Menocal contended that it did not preclude other forms of "secular" identification, particularly in al-Andalus during the Umayyad rule from the eighth through the early eleventh centuries.[14] It may have proved an important mode of affiliation in the Islamicate trade system, although analysis is inconclusive. Constable argued that religion was so crucial a mark of identity that traders of the three faiths tended to bond with their brethren in partnership arrangements. Although geographic affiliation was generally strong among Andalusi merchants of all religions, she maintained that religious and "ethnic" similarities were more important than geography, claiming that interfaith partnerships were also rare.[15] Despite the paucity of these formal interfaith partnerships in Constable's work, scholars of the Geniza documents generally emphasize that Jewish merchants indeed partnered with Muslims and hired non-Jewish agents, as in the case of Yūsuf b. 'Awkal, who corresponded with his Muslim agents in Arabic script.[16] Most of Ibn 'Awkal's agents were not employees, but were other traders working without pay because they sought reciprocal services from the prestigious House of Ibn 'Awkal. Evidence shows that Ibn 'Awkal also conducted business with Christian merchants from Alexandria.[17] Examples from other facets of the commercial environment contradict generalizations about "ethnic" or religious exclusivity among traders; in late fifteenth-century Valencia, for example, much of that city's mercantile success at that time was due to Valencia's *mudéjares*, who enjoyed close relations with Jewish and Christian merchants. Manuel Ruzafa García demonstrates that many *mudéjar* merchants were saved during an attack on Valencia's Muslim quarter (*morería*) in 1455 when their Christian colleagues provisionally took them into their homes.[18] Religion sometimes was an important factor in identity construction, although frequently it seemed to play no significant role. Examining networked interactions between different communities helps to expand the supposed stability of the term "religion," to question generalizations about interfaith relations, and to generate new ways to describe them.

Other modern terms, such as "ethnicity," "race," and "national" identity, may have played a role in differentiating western trader communities from one another in the eleventh- and twelfth-century Mediterranean economic milieu. Merchants from Genoa, Pisa, Barcelona, and Marseilles, for example, opposed being merged into one large faction in the institutional system of merchant hostelries and warehouses called *fondacos* (ar. *fanādiq*), as discussed in chapter 4. The early Islamicate *fanādiq* often differentiated among professional, commercial, and regional clusters, so that the segregation of regional or perhaps urban groups in their own later *fondacos* from the twelfth century on was not completely novel.[19] Constable maintained that it is difficult to know whether such divisions were due to local law, or to travellers' preferences.[20] Although Constable referred to these distinctions as nominally "national," proposals by Robert Bartlett and Tabish Khair, who claim that medieval ethnicity was constituted by language, mores, dress, law, and customs, rather than by race in the modern, bodily sense, offer a wider scope for analysis. Patrick Geary concurs, adding that ethnicity is a mental creation.[21] Elizabeth Isichei contends that ethnicity was forged in large part in non-modern North Africa by ecological factors, meaning that group association occurred through crops, livelihood, and agricultural production, rather than consanguinity.[22] Hence, non-modern people identified with one another not in accordance with "nations" as we understand them today, but based on common languages, customs, discourses, and daily work routines. This is especially evident prior to the eleventh and twelfth centuries, when people were not identified with kings, kingdoms, or spheres of influence, but with the very practices that bound them as Asturians or Portuguese.[23]

Non-modern Cultural Polarities

Network theory and WSA help to envision and examine culture and identity as a system of continuities and deviations, a method that finds echoes in Glick's theory of a dominant "Andalusi cultural polarity." Glick argued that a preponderant Andalusi cultural mode prevailed in medieval Iberia until substantial aid from monks at Cluny and later Cîteaux began to effect major shifts in Castile and León starting in the eleventh century with the construction of churches and monasteries.[24] Cluny's influence led to the implementation of Gregorian reforms and a dramatic rise in the numbers of bishops and bishoprics in Hispanicate domains by 1150. Hispanicate kingdoms were recast to fit European models, which included the change from the Mozarabic to the Roman liturgy, facilitated by monks from Cluny. The parallel between territorial kingship in Hispanicate realms (*regalia territorial*) and the Islamicate political structure exemplifies how the Hispanicate kingdoms appeared more Andalusi than European as a result of the dominant Andalusi cultural polarity: "The notion of a territorial kingship (*regalia territorial*), though inherited from the Visigothic juridical tradition was nevertheless reinforced by the example of Islamic norms prevalent in al-Andalus."[25] Examining Andalusi and Hispanicate cultures as part of the same Iberian system allows for discussions of interconnection between them, rather than focusing on separation and antagonism.

Network theory and WSA provide a frame for the sort of royal and cultural intersection proposed by Maribel Fierro and Ana M. Montero in their work on the cultural project of Alfonso X, which in turn suggests a reformulation of the "Andalusi cultural polarity" as theorized by Glick. Fierro extends Montero's analysis of the similarities between passages in Alfonso's *Setenario* and Ibn Ṭufayl's twelfth-century *Risālat Ḥayy ibn Yaqẓān fi asrār al-ḥikma l-mashriqiyya* composed at the Almohad court, to argue that the Almohad project of sapience, which was to ultimately achieve "a radical political transformation," served as the framework for Alfonso X's political and cultural goals.[26] Fierro identifies the parallels between the monarchic cultural project of the Almohad caliphs, who ruled the Maghreb and al-Andalus from 1147 until 1269, and Alfonso X's renowned political, intellectual, and artistic plans as ruler of Castile from 1252 to 1284. Far from an indication of mere "influence" of Islamicate culture on the Hispanicate king, Fierro suggests that Andalusi cultural models continued as the standard for Hispanicate rulers such as Alfonso X, at the same time that al-Andalus no longer wielded the same political power as before. Fierro's and Montero's work also signals the absence of an ostensible separation between the "Andalusi cultural polarity" and the Hispanicate or Castilian one, as if the Andalusi polarity somehow existed in a different time and space than that of Alfonso X. In other words, Fierro asks to what degree was Alfonso "the last Almohad caliph" and not merely a Castilian king operating according to the paradigms of another culture? To what extent were the models that Alfonso relied on those of his own culture, and not of al-Andalus? Network and system principles compel scholars to think about al-Andalus as Alfonso's own cultural referent in the Iberian cultural system, and not as "foreign" to Alfonso's supposedly different, Castilian culture.[27]

Cynthia Robinson offers a precedent to the link between Alfonso X and the Almohads in her work on the connections between Andalusi and Provençal culture in the eleventh century, specifically her exploration of the correspondence of their courtly lyric production. Robinson contends that neither culture was pre-eminent in the development of the courtly lyric during the eleventh century; rather, their linguistic differences aside, they were one and the same. Robinson avoids trying to determine the origins of the so-called troubadour lyric, and instead asserts that the court cultures of the Andalusi *ṭā'ifa* kingdoms and Provence were largely identical. She maintains the "similarity and interpenetration between Zaragozan and Provençal court cultures during most of the eleventh century and the earliest decades of the twelfth."[28] Rosa María Rodríguez Porto calls for recognition of a similar relationship between the court cultures of fourteenth-century Castile and Granada, whose artistic exchange prompted shared chivalric iconography and imagery in manuscripts and the Alhambra's Hall of Justice. Rodríguez Porto draws on networked political and cultural alliances throughout the thirteenth and fourteenth centuries, thus implicitly demonstrating fluid relations between artists, diplomats, and politicians in different kingdoms of the Iberian system.[29] These scholars above cited indicate that connections between the cultural systems of Castile, Provence, and al-Andalus were complex and shifting, rather than static and antagonistic, demonstrating cultural resemblance and sameness in many cases, rather than difference.

Hispanicate pilgrimage and *ḥajj* exemplify and reinforce the networked relations between Andalusi and Hispanicate cultures. In chapter 4 we saw that four practices overlapped along non-modern travel routes, including *ḥajj* or pilgrimage, commerce and trade, saints' veneration, and educational or cultural travel. Examining Iberian pilgrimage as an interfaith system with destinations in Santiago de Compostela and Mecca is in accord with Sylvia Chiffoleau and Anna Madoeuf's argument about the pilgrimage gesture overall, which they claim is inscribed in a genealogy that harks back to Jewish tradition, repeated by Christianity and its cult of the patron saint, as well as by the Muslim obligation of *ḥajj*.[30] Pilgrimage was an effective tool for the construction of collective identities, which is evident in the similarity between travel routes in the Islamicate and Latinate worlds. José Luis Barreiro Rivas has described them as "emerging spaces" with activities geared toward the creation of collective identities and symbolic links between subjects and power.[31]

In the non-modern Islamicate travel system, *ḥajj* is a well-known and even coveted obligation of the Muslim faithful, though it has not inevitably confirmed the unity of the *umma* or Islamic community through time. Instead, it has played varying historical roles in collective and individual identity formation. M.E. McMillan argues that, beginning with Muhammad's successors after his death, it became important as an opportunity for leaders to demonstrate their guidance of their community and to "enhance their political legitimacy."[32] From the eighth to the eleventh century the Umayyads in Cordova employed it as a means to dignify themselves and their territory in their rivalry with historically more prestigious centres and rulers in Damascus, Cairo, and 'Abbāsid Baghdad, demonstrating fragmentation in the large-scale Islamic identification of the *umma*, and more consolidated, discrete identity on a smaller, geo-dynastic scale. Dominique Urvoy highlights *ḥajj*'s growth as a way for the Umayyads to differentiate themselves from the more prestigious North African and Middle Eastern locales, while Ian Richard Netton concurs, claiming that *ḥajj* in the Umayyad period was motivated by the rivalry between the upstart Andalus in the west and the intellectual and political hubs in the east, indicating that the Andalusis encouraged *ḥajj* as a way to compete with their cultural and political adversaries.[33] Thus, *ḥajj* reinforced collective identities and links between rulers and subjects within particular network nodes, such as Cordova, although its impact clearly extended in the larger network to peoples and communities beyond single nodes or spheres, as in the rivalry between Umayyad Cordova and 'Abbāsid Baghdad. *Ḥajj* consolidated the political power of local Umayyad authorities in al-Andalus, though the shaping of identity through pilgrimage depended on pilgrims' participation in the activities.

Relations of power are also evident in pilgrimage and collective identities along the Camino de Santiago. The Camino's construction began in earnest in the twelfth century, in order to promote Compostela as a destination for seekers of relics, although José Luis Barreiro Rivas and Francisco Márquez Villanueva situate its development within the larger goals of western secular rulers and the papacy in Rome to centralize political and religious values in western Christendom. Barreiro Rivas argues that Rome and the Christian west were more concerned with their Byzantine rivals in the east than with Islam, despite the political and economic rivalry between the Islamic empire and European kingdoms in the west.[34] Hence, the Camino's growth in the twelfth and thirteenth centuries coincided with more general European political and papal expansion.

Travel for the purpose of saint veneration was a frequent activity that allowed authorities to consolidate political and cultural power. Peter Brown proposed that the growth of Christian travel to shrines emerged generally with the rise of relics, which were linked to specific places and subsequently enhanced the power of bishops in those areas. The wedding of ecclesiastical authority to "the tombs of the dead" distinguished the Catholic west from its eastern neighbours, whether Christians, Jews, or Muslims, because as Brown argues Christian pilgrimage and saint veneration in the eastern Mediterranean and Near East (including Jerusalem) never came to support ecclesiastical power structures as they did in the west.[35] Relics and saint veneration in the west thus effectively contributed to political goals, and to the creation of western Christian subjects who were different not only from Christians in the east, but also from Muslims and Jews.[36]

Examining Iberian pilgrimage as a multicultural, Iberian system, rather than as Christian or Muslim, allows for comparative and contrastive analysis of their parallels and differences. But the network/system model permits even more analytical depth. In accord with Fierro's hypothesis about the Andalusi cultural model of Alfonso X, I have argued that it is possible that Hispanicate and European authorities began to construct the Camino de Santiago with the North African travel system and *ḥajj* to Mecca as models.[37] I maintained that the Camino's rise constituted an honorific imitation of the Islamicate models, which integrated al-Andalus in their networks and preceded the Iberian pilgrimage routes by approximately 200 years. The convergence of religion, politics, and economic and cultural exchange, which forged the Camino's identity and success,[38] also wholly characterized the North African roads and their proposed culmination in Mecca. The Camino was renowned for travel for these varied purposes, from the many local pilgrimages to shrines and churches to the cultural diffusion of manuscripts, architectural styles, and songs.[39] It is possible that the Camino resembled the Maghribi routes because Iberia was part of the Islamicate world to varying degrees throughout the Middle Ages. Familiarity with the prestigious North African network would have permitted Hispanicate authorities to take advantage of its proximity and eventually surpass its reputation. The Camino's successful growth overlapped with the gradual consolidation and shift in Iberian political and economic power from Andalusi to Hispanicate kingdoms during the twelfth and thirteenth centuries.[40] Further research on the interconnected network of *ḥajj* and pilgrimage would continue to illuminate the standards involved in their dialectic, constitutive negotiation in non-modern Iberia. Examining non-modern Iberian culture as a system obviates the reliance on static, delimited cultural categories.

Epilogue

Applications of network theory and World-Systems Analysis (WSA) have a reach far beyond the themes explored briefly in these final chapters, since the methods and models allow us to better edge toward Iberia than traditional ideological and methodological paradigms. A gamut of literary and cultural themes are pertinent, ranging from the multilingual medieval love system identified by María Rosa Menocal, to the non-modern literary network explored by David A. Wacks.[1] Networks and systems propel analysis beyond the conventional limits of our disciplines.

Literary scholars and historians whose work is wide ranging and who aim to minimize linguistic and disciplinary boundaries inspire further interrogation of our fields. Scholarly resources also offer inroads to more expansive approaches. Entries in the *Encyclopedia of Islam* make surprising connections at times between themes that have traditionally been held apart, as in the entry for the Andalusi Arabic *zajal* poem. The authors assert the appearance of certain of the *zajal*'s techniques in romance literature, including the *Libro de buen amor*, and perhaps more remarkably, "in the service of religion" in Alfonso X's *Cantigas de Santa María*.[2] These poetic crossings, from an often caustic and ludic Andalusi *zajal* genre to miracle poems of the Virgin in the *Cantigas*, challenge the religious and cultural divides traditionally applied to non-modern Iberian literatures, divides between al-Andalus and Castile, the secular and the sacred, and Arabic language and romance. Network theory and WSA certainly provide frameworks for linking different Iberian poetic genres in Arabic and romance. They may even convert unexpected statements about the *zajal* into common knowledge that we integrate in our research and teaching, compelling us to bring together readings and translations from different linguistic and cultural traditions in our classrooms and scholarship.

Yet the broader contributions of network theory and WSA stretch beyond specific topics to the larger realm of cultural theory. Recent assessments in non-modern Iberian studies, including Menocal's love system or Josiah Blackmore and Gregory S. Hutcheson's examination of sexuality in *Queer Iberia: Sexualities, Cultures and Crossings from the Middle Ages to the Renaissance*, based their ideas on the disruption of rigid categories and structures. For instance, the love system hinged on abandoning the idea of al-Andalus, North Africa, Catalunya, Aragon, and Provence as rigidly bound, hermetic spaces that would prohibit poetry's transregional flows. Likewise, Blackmore and Hutcheson's study of Iberian sexuality turned on a broader critique of the stability of Spanish identity, which enabled fluid queer interpretations of non-modern texts.[3] Network theory and WSA complement such work and go beyond the post-Foucauldian questioning of categories, especially through the feature of relationality that stands out as so crucial in the models. Network theory and WSA fill the gap created by the dismantling of stable, rigid classifications and compel a focus on the interaction and relations between shifting phenomena, as we have seen.[4]

A plethora of themes invite the application of the relationality implicit in network theory and WSA, such as the familiar topics of Iberian gender and sexuality, or the non-modern Iberian body more generally intrinsic to and embedded in discourses of medicine, well-being, and law. Scholars could adopt broad, macro perspectives to link these topics in Iberia to other non-modern realms, or assume more limited micro lenses to investigate smaller, restricted systems. The vast cultural production of the so-called gender debates on women and men from the fourteenth to the eighteenth centuries is suited to the application of network and system methods and models, since it encompassed a variety of interlinking works from religious, literary, and medical genres, produced in a range of locales in Iberia and Europe. Network theory and WSA provide tools to explore not only the intersections and overlaps between works in the textual system and their constructions of bodies and gender, but also between the cultural system and political networks fundamental to the books' production. These imbricated political and textual networks compel further research on how their interactions contributed to the production and reinforcement of, and change in attitudes about men and women over a long period, or even a more limited time.[5]

And finally, the interrelations essential to network theory and WSA encourage the analysis of topics that extend beyond cultural theory or a defined cultural theme to larger questions of societal inequity and disjuncture. The theories allow greater dexterity in relating networks and phenomena that contribute to the sort of disjointed, vertiginous reality today in which human rights do not correspond to socio-economic rights, in which broad shifts in attitudes about gay marriage and the rights of transgender and transsexual people do not coincide with greater socio-economic equality. On the contrary, at the same time that many countries and communities increasingly recognize and legitimize gender and sexual diversity, socio-economic inequality is exacerbated and progressively more entrenched.[6] Network theory and WSA provide methods and tools for greater analytical breadth in these and many other topics.

Notes

Introduction

1 Marshall G.S. Hodgson proposed the term "Islamicate" to refer to a common culture among people of different backgrounds, in *The Venture of Islam: Conscience and History in a World Civilization*. I use Islamicate, Hispanicate, and Christianate as a way to interrogate the use of religious, ethnic, and cultural absolutes to characterize blended and diverse political, social, and economic orders throughout the non-modern world.
2 Thomas F. Glick counters these problematic tendencies in *Islamic and Christian Spain in the Early Middle Ages*, xv–xx.
3 Ray A. Kea, "Expansions and Contractions: World-Historical Change and the Western Sudan World-System (1200/1000 BC–1200/1250 AD)," 724; María Jesús Viguera Molins, "Al-Andalus y oriente: crónica de una historia compartida," 36.
4 Just as Wallerstein argues that scholars would benefit from explicitly considering the history, structure, contradictions, and prospects of today's capitalist world-economy, scholars of the past would gain from greater overt attention to those topics in the non-modern world, Immanuel Wallerstein, "Thinking about the 'Humanities,'" 226.
5 R. Howard Bloch and Stephen G. Nichols, eds., *Medievalism and the Modernist Temper*, 25–30. For the role of Ramón Menéndez Pidal in the invention of the Middle Ages in nineteenth-century Spain, see Catherine Brown, "The Relics of Menéndez Pidal: Mourning and Melancholia in Hispanomedieval Studies."
6 Kathleen Davis and Nadia Altschul, "The Idea of 'the Middle Ages' Outside Europe," 8.
7 María Rosa Menocal, "Why Iberia?," 7–11.

8 Peter Linehan, "At the Spanish Frontier," 40.

9 Eloy Martín Corrales, *La imagen del magrebí en España: una perspectiva histórica, siglos XVI–XX.*

10 The Spanish diplomat Máximo Cajal studied the fraught topic of Spain's definition and used the question "Where does Spain end?" as his point of departure, in *Ceuta, Melilla, Olivenza, Gibraltar. ¿Dónde acaba España?*

11 Muslims dominated Mediterranean trade from the tenth through twelfth centuries, though realignments occurred in the thirteenth and fourteenth centuries with new associations between Islamicate and European realms, Olivia Remie Constable, *Trade and Traders in Muslim Spain*; and, Javier Brun, dir., Joaquín Benito, and Pedro Canut, *Redes culturales: claves para sobrevivir en la globalización*, 68.

12 Oystein S. LaBianca and Sandra Arnold Scham, "Introduction: Ancient Network Societies."

13 Kea, "Expansions and Contractions;" Janet L. Abu-Lughod, *Before European Hegemony: The World System A.D. 1250–1350.*

14 Ross E. Dunn, *The Adventures of Ibn Battuta: A Muslim Traveler of the Fourteenth Century*, ix; miriam cooke and Bruce B. Lawrence, "Introduction," 10.

15 Nayan Chanda, *Bound Together: How Traders, Preachers, Adventurers, and Warriors Shaped Globalization*, 32.

16 David Held, Anthony McGrew, David Goldblatt, and Jonathan Perraton, *Global Transformations: Politics, Economics, and Culture*, 415–35.

17 Jürgen Osterhammel and Niels P. Petersson, *Globalization: A Short History*, 27–8.

18 Eduardo Manzano Moreno compares the institutional character of Hispanicate kingdoms in the eleventh and twelfth century to the more informal networks in al-Andalus, *Historia de España: épocas medievales*, vol. 2, 333–7.

19 Janina M. Safran calls the idea of univocal Islamic law "misleading" when referring to the three centuries after the arrival of Muslims in al-Andalus, since legal notions such as Dār al-ḥarb and Dār al-Islām were constantly in debate, *Defining Boundaries in al-Andalus: Muslims, Christians, and Jews in Islamic Iberia*, 19.

20 Zoroastrianism is a Central Asian religion whose devotees from Iran and India worship the sanctified poet Zarathushtra, or Zoroaster. It was the main religion of Iranians from the Achaemenid (550–330 BCE) through the Sassanīd dynasty (224–650 CE), the latter contemporaneous with the advent of Islam in the seventh century CE, Jamsheed K. Choksy, "Zoroastrianism."

21 A. Abel, "Dār al-Ḥarb," 126; A. Abel, "Dār al-Islām," 127; J. Robson, "Ḥadīth," 23.
22 J. Schacht, "Aḥkām," 256.
23 Safran, *Defining Boundaries*, 169.
24 Immanuel Wallerstein, *Historical Capitalism* with *Capitalist Civilization*, 89. See Gopal Balakrishnan for further discussion, in "The Twilight of Capital?," 232.
25 Constable, *Trade and Traders*.
26 The economist Karl Polanyi recognized that systems generally operate with three principles of exchange, although the dominant principle governs the means of production, in *Primitive, Archaic, and Modern Economies: Essays of Karl Polanyi*, 1968. Polanyi does not argue here that the economic domain is autonomous from social and historical realms, a concept that Marxist anthropologists and others routinely criticize as a way to reinforce the principles of neoliberal capitalism. For a recent denunciation of economic autonomy, see Judith Butler and Athena Athanasiou, *Dispossession: The Performative in the Political*, 38–43.
27 Tabish Khair, "African and Asian Travel Texts in the Light of Europe: An Introduction," 4; Glick, *Islamic and Christian Spain*, 13–14.
28 Amitov Ghosh, *In an Antique Land*, 157. See *Corpus of Early Arabic Sources for West African History* and *Libros españoles de viajes medievales (selección)* for journeys ranging from the diplomatic to the economic.
29 S.D. Goitein, *A Mediterranean Society: The Jewish Communities of the Arab World as Portrayed in the Documents of the Cairo Geniza*, vol. 3, 61–2. The name al-Dimyātī links Ḥalfōn ben Nathanel to the Egyptian port of Dumyāt or Damietta.
30 "El mundo medieval no fue un mundo cerrado, sino que fue recorrido una y otra vez," 11.
31 Osterhammel and Petersson, *Globalization: A Short History*, 27–8.
32 Khair, "African," 18.
33 Susan Reynolds, "Society: Hierarchy and Solidarity," 94–115.
34 Polanyi, *Primitive, Archaic, and Modern Economies*, 3–27.
35 Glick, *Islamic and Christian Spain*, xv–xx.
36 Ibid., xvii, 226–7, 244; Miquel Barceló, *Arqueología medieval en las afueras del "medievalismo."*
37 Manuela Marín questions the similarity of medieval and modern "slavery" in *Al-Ándalus y los andalusíes*, 45–6, as does Eduardo Manzano Moreno, *Historia de las sociedades musulmanas en la Edad Media*, 192–3.
38 Moses I. Finley, *Ancient Slavery and Modern Ideology*, 136–7.
39 For the connection between poverty and modern global capitalism, see Joseph E. Stiglitz, *Globalization and Its Discontents*, ix, 4–8.

40 Carmen López Alonso mentions the ambiguity of medieval Iberian poverty in *La pobreza en la España medieval: estudio histórico-social*, 19, 638.
41 Ibid., 69.
42 S.D. Goitein, *Jews and Arabs: Their Contacts Through the Ages*, 188.
43 Benedict Anderson, *Imagined Communities: Reflections on the Origin and Spread of Nationalism*; James Casey, *Early Modern Spain: A Social History*, 1; Teófilo F. Ruiz, *Spanish Society, 1400–1600*, 11.
44 Eduardo Manzano Moreno, "Christian-Muslim Frontier in Al-Andalus: Idea and Reality," especially 83–4.
45 Judith Butler, *Gender Trouble: Feminism and the Subversion of Identity*.
46 Manzano Moreno argues that Pelayo's lineage was Asturian, not Gothic, in "Christian-Muslim Frontier," 90–1.
47 Américo Castro, *España en su historia: cristianos, moros y judíos*.

1 Periodization and Geography

1 Historical revisions include Eduardo Manzano Moreno, "Christian-Muslim Frontier in Al-Andalus: Idea and Reality"; Joseph F. O'Callaghan, *Reconquest and Crusade in Medieval Spain*; Amira K. Bennison, "The Peoples of the North in the Eyes of the Muslims of Umayyad al-Andalus (711–1031)"; and Francisco García Fitz, *Reconquista*.
2 Barbara Fuchs, "1492 and the Cleaving of Hispanism"; *Exotic Nation: Maurophilia and the Construction of Early Modern Spain*, 32–3.
3 José Antonio Maravall, *Antiguos y modernos: la idea de progreso en el desarrollo inicial de una sociedad*, 285.
4 Alfonso X, ed. Benito Brancaforte, *Prosa histórica*, 45–51, 103–4.
5 Kathleen Davis, *Periodization and Sovereignty: How Ideas of Feudalism and Secularization Govern the Politics of Time*, 1–20, 135n5. Davis claims that studies by historians such as Jacques Le Goff are pivotal in consolidating the idea of cyclical and preordained time as normative in the Middle Ages, Le Goff, *Time, Work, and Culture in the Middle Ages*, 29–52.
6 Margreta de Grazia, "The Modern Divide: From Either Side," 453.
7 Maravall, *Antiguos y modernos*; Fernando García de Cortázar and José Manuel González Vesga, *Breve historia de España*, 337–417.
8 Norman F. Cantor, *Inventing the Middle Ages*; John Dagenais, *The Ethics of Reading in Manuscript Culture*; Umberto Eco, *Travels in Hyperreality: Essays*; Mark D. Meyerson, "Introduction," xii–xiv; Gabrielle M. Spiegel, *Past as Text*.
9 Kathleen Davis and Nadia Altschul, "The Idea of 'the Middle Ages' Outside Europe," 21; Davis, *Periodization and Sovereignty*, 20.

10 Ania Loomba, "Periodization, Race, and Global Contact," 596.
11 Jennifer Summit and David Wallace, "Rethinking Periodization," 449–50.
12 Daniel Martin Varisco, "Making 'Medieval' Islam Meaningful," especially 389–94.
13 Ibid., 386, 403, 410–11.
14 Eco, *Travels in Hyperreality*, 69, 71.
15 Simon R. Doubleday, "'Criminal Non-Intervention:' Hispanism, Medievalism, and the Pursuit of Neutrality," 7.
16 José Rabasa, "Decolonizing Medieval Mexico," 27–32. Fuchs discusses the year 1492 as the end of an era, in "1492 and the Cleaving of Hispanism."
17 Manuel De Landa, *A Thousand Years of Nonlinear History*, 21–2.
18 Rabasa briefly addresses this issue in the context of modern India, "Decolonizing Medieval Mexico," 30.
19 María Rosa Menocal, *Shards of Love: Exile and the Origins of the Lyric*, 200.
20 Kathleen Biddick, "The Cut of Pedagogy: Genealogy in the Blood," 459.
21 María Rosa Menocal, *Writing in Dante's Cult of Truth: From Borges to Boccaccio*, 3.
22 Paul Freedman, "Spanish March," 761. José Antonio Maravall defines the *marca* as an unstable, imprecise zone lacking both a fixed organization and the presence of a certain, focused administrative power ("La 'marca,' por su propia naturaleza, alude a una zona inestable, imprecisa, sin organización fija, sin que se dé en ella la presencia de un poder seguro y administrativamente canalizado"), *Estado moderno y mentalidad social (siglos XV a XVII)*, vol. 1, 121.
23 Anthony Pym, *Negotiating the Frontier: Translators and Intercultures in Hispanic History*, 15.
24 Jorge Lirola Delgado, "El tráfico marítimo de la Almería andalusí (siglos X–XII)," 109. Marc Bloch presented similar findings with slightly different details, in *La société féodale: la formation des liens de dépendance*, 13–16.
25 Philippe Sénac, *Los soberanos carolingios y al-Andalus (siglos VIII–IX)*, 161; Abū 'Abd Allāh Muhammad Ibn 'Abd al-Mun'im al-Ḥimyarī, *Kitāb al-Rawd al-Mi'tar* (The Book of the Fragrant Gardens), 16.
26 García de Cortázar and González Vesga, *Breve historia de España*, 130.
27 Isidoro de Sevilla, *Etimologías*, vol. 2, chap. 14, 4.29.
28 Jean Dangler, "Edging Toward Iberia," 14. Gerald R. Tibbetts asserts that North Africa "includes Spain" on al-Iṣṭakhrī's map, suggesting that the mapmaker reckoned the two areas together as one, in J.B. Harley and David Woodward, eds., *The History of Cartography*, vol. 2, bk. 1, 114, 119.
29 *Other Routes: 1500 Years of African and Asian Travel Writing*, 54. Daniele Grammatico contends that this entire Maghribi zone was connected to the

Dār al-Islām, or the Domain of Islam at the height of Muslim domination in al-Andalus, "El Magreb y al-Andalus: una historia humana entretejida," 18–19. Elizabeth Isichei calls Qayrawān in present-day Tunisia the centre of a great province that comprised the eastern Maghreb and al-Andalus, or in other words all of North Africa and Iberia, *A History of African Societies to 1870*, 176.

30 Manuela Marín, *Al-Ándalus y los andalusíes*, 13: "La realidad andalusí, por tanto, es un concepto geográficamente variable y sometido a una disminución constante desde el siglo XI en adelante."

31 Ralph Penny, *History of the Spanish Language*, 30; María Rosa Menocal, "Visions of al-Andalus," 12.

32 Menocal, "Visions," 12.

33 José Antonio Maravall, *El concepto de España en la Edad Media*, 26–7.

34 Ibid., 43: "España es, para nuestros historiadores medievales, una entidad humana asentada en un territorio que la define y caracteriza y a la cual le sucede algo en común, toda una historia propia."

35 Ibid., 556–7.

36 Isidoro, *Etimologías*, vol. 2, chap. 14, 4.28.

37 The cultural anthropologists Sharon R. Roseman and Shawn S. Parkhurst use "Iberia" specifically to challenge notions of space and culture through time, "Culture and Space in Iberian Anthropology," 2, 6–7.

38 For an overview of critical approaches to the term from the late nineteenth century, see Nora Berend, "Preface," x–xv. For early uses and meanings of the frontier, see Peter Linehan, "At the Spanish Frontier," 37–8, and Frederick Jackson Turner, "The Significance of the Frontier in American History," 1–50.

39 Linehan, "Spanish Frontier," 39, 53.

40 David Abulafia, "Introduction: Seven Types of Ambiguity, c. 1100–c. 1500," 1–3, 34. Alberto Montaner Frutos calls the medieval frontier a mood, an attitude about life, and a state of mind ("la frontera era en el Medievo un estado de ánimo, una actitud vital, una mentalidad"), "Un canto de frontera: geopolítica y geopoética del *Cantar de mio Cid*," 8.

41 José Mattoso, *História de Portugal*, vol. 2, *A Monarquia Feudal (1096–1480)*, 19. Montaner Frutos agrees that the frontier never was a line, but rather an area, "Canto," 8.

42 Linehan, "Spanish Frontier," 49; Manzano Moreno, "Christian-Muslim Frontier," 96.

43 Ronnie Ellenblum, "Borders and Borderlines in the Middle Ages? The Example of the Latin Kingdom of Jerusalem," 111.

44 Ibid., 108.

45 Ibid., 109–10.

46 Gilles Deleuze and Félix Guattari, *Anti-Oedipus: Capitalism and Schizophrenia*; Eve Kosofsky Sedgwick, *Between Men: English Literature and Male Homosocial Desire.*

2 Network Theory and World-Systems Analysis

1 According to Javier Brun, Joaquín Benito, and Pedro Canut: "Las redes han existido, como formas de organización desde hace mucho tiempo" [Networks have existed as forms of organization for a long time], *Redes culturales: claves para sobrevivir en la globalización*, 67.

2 Manuel Castells, ed., *The Network Society: A Cross-Cultural Perspective*, 3–7; and, Manuel Castells, *The Internet Galaxy: Reflections on the Internet, Business, and Society*, 1–2.

3 Manuel Castells, *Communication Power*, 20.

4 Ibid., 21.

5 Ibid., 21; Castells, *Network Society*, 4.

6 Brun, Benito, and Canut, *Redes culturales*, 33–4.

7 Oystein S. LaBianca and Sandra Arnold Scham, "Introduction: Ancient Network Societies," 1.

8 Ibid., 2.

9 Manuel Castells, "Nothing New Under the Sun?," 158–9.

10 Ibid., 159–60. Although he does not overtly insist on historical contextualization in his book, *Communication Power*, Castells clearly describes the framework of today's global network society, in contrast to networks in the past, especially 21–7.

11 Castells, "Nothing New," 160–1; Castells, *Communication Power*, 23.

12 LaBianca and Arnold Scham, "Introduction," 2, 5.

13 Castells, *Communication Power*, 21–2.

14 Ibid., 22.

15 LaBianca and Arnold Scham, "Introduction," 2.

16 Castells cites and concurs with Mitchell's estimation of developments in information and communication technology, in *Communication Power*, 23–4. See William J. Mitchell, *Me++: The Cyborg Self and the Networked City*. Castells further explains his claims about the critical importance of modern technology in "Nothing New," 161–3.

17 David Singh Grewal, *Network Power: The Social Dynamics of Globalization*, 18, 20.

18 Ibid., 5.

19 LaBianca and Arnold Scham, "Introduction," 2.

20 Castells, *Communication Power*, 34. Neil Brenner condemns "space of flows" when he agrees with critics who argue that it obscures the real aims of corporations to remove the processes related to the production and movement of capital from conventional places, such as cities, nations, and regions, in an effort to avoid regulatory oversight and constraints, "The Space of the World: Beyond State-Centrism?," 121, 125.
21 LaBianca and Arnold Scham, "Introduction," 2.
22 Castells, *Communication Power*, 19, 40.
23 Ibid., 40. Brenner advocates for revising notions of the state from a world-systems perspective and calls for research on "rescaling the state," in "Space of the World," especially, 126–33.
24 Castells, *Communication Power*, 40–1.
25 Singh Grewal, *Network Power*, 234.
26 Ibid., 50.
27 Castells, *Communication Power*, 41.
28 P. Nick Kardulias, "World-Systems Applications for Understanding the Bronze Age in the Eastern Mediterranean," 54.
29 Immanuel Wallerstein, *World-Systems Analysis: An Introduction*, 23.
30 Kardulias, "World-Systems Applications," 56. For this general description of World-Systems Analysis, I also rely on Wallerstein, *World-Systems Analysis*, and on William Parkinson and Michael L. Galaty, "Introduction: Interaction and Ancient Societies," 3–28.
31 Kardulias, "World-Systems Applications," 56.
32 Wallerstein, *World-Systems Analysis*, 93.
33 Ibid., 11; and, Kardulias, "World-Systems Applications," 56.
34 Wallerstein, *World-Systems Analysis*, 12.
35 Ibid., 14–15.
36 Fernand Braudel, *The Mediterranean and the Mediterranean World in the Age of Phillip II.*
37 Wallerstein, *World-Systems Analysis*, 17.
38 David Palumbo-Liu, Bruce Robbins, and Nirvana Tanoukhi, eds. *Immanuel Wallerstein and the Problem of the World: System, Scale, Culture.*
39 Janet L. Abu-Lughod, *Before European Hegemony: The World System A.D. 1250–1350*, 33–6.
40 Ibid., 11–12.
41 Ibid., 18.
42 Olivia Remie Constable, "Foreword," xix–xx.
43 Ibid., xx.
44 Gene W. Heck's recent study contrasts with Abu-Lughod's reticence on

early links to modern capitalism. Heck contends that "a distinct early form of commercial capitalism slowly, but inexorably, evolved in the marketplaces of the medieval Islamic Empire," *Charlemagne, Muhammad, and the Arab Roots of Capitalism*, 4.

45 Abu-Lughod, *Before European Hegemony*, 11.

46 Ibid., 9–13.

47 Enrique D. Dussel, "World-System and 'Trans'-Modernity," 224.

48 Ray A. Kea, "Expansions and Contractions: World-Historical Change and the Western Sudan World-System (1200/1000BC–1200/1250AD)," 724–5.

49 Ibid., 801.

50 Ibid., 726.

51 Ibid., 731–2.

52 Ibid., 732–4, 801.

53 Richard E. Lee, "The Modern World-System: Its Structures, Its Geoculture, Its Crisis and Transformation," 39.

54 Parkinson and Galaty, "Introduction," 25–6.

55 David Palumbo-Liu, Bruce Robbins, and Nirvana Tanoukhi, "Introduction: The Most Important Thing Happening," 11; Parkinson and Galaty, "Introduction," 9, 11, 23.

56 Palumbo-Liu, Robbins, and Tanoukhi, "Introduction," 11.

3 The Islamicate Trade Network

1 Thomas F. Glick, *Islamic and Christian Spain in the Early Middle Ages*, 14. S.D. Goitein considered the Mediterranean a "free-trade community," *A Mediterranean Society: The Jewish Communities of the Arab World as Portrayed in the Documents of the Cairo Geniza*, vol. 1, 61.

2 Avner Greif, *Institutions and the Path to the Modern Economy: Lessons from Medieval Trade*, 61. Greif defines the Jewish merchants of the Cairo Geniza as a "Maghribi" coalition, although Jeremy Edwards and Sheilagh Ogilvie dispute their exclusivity, in "Contract Enforcement, Institutions, and Social Capital: The Maghribi Traders Reappraised," 421–3. Jessica L. Goldberg disagrees as well, in *Trade and Institutions in the Medieval Mediterranean: The Geniza Merchants and Their Business World*, 12–13, 41–2, 44–5 and passim.

3 Glick, *Islamic and Christian Spain*, 14; Goitein, *Mediterranean Society*, vol. 1, 275.

4 Olivia Remie Constable, *Trade and Traders in Muslim Spain: The Commercial Realignment of the Iberian Peninsula, 900–1500*, 16; Glick, *Islamic and Christian Spain*, 136.

5 Constable, *Trade and Traders*, 16–23.
6 Glick, *Islamic and Christian Spain*, 138–9.
7 Constable, *Trade and Traders*, 30–1, 31n49.
8 Ibid., 35–6.
9 Ibid., chapter 4, and 79–80.
10 Ibid., 201, 201n156; Elizabeth Isichei, *A History of African Societies to 1870*, 178–9.
11 Ralph A. Austen, *African Economic History: Internal Development and External Dependency*, 34.
12 Philippe Sénac, "Le Maghreb al-Aqsā et l'Occident chrétien (VIIIe–IXe siècles)," 20.
13 Florin Curta, "Markets in Tenth-Century al-Andalus and Volga Bulghāria: Contrasting Views of Trade in Muslim Europe," 306–7n8; Pedro Chalmeta, *El zoco medieval: contribución al estudio de la historia del mercado*, 454; Manuel Acién Almansa, "Poblamiento y sociedad en al-Andalus: un mundo de ciudades, alquerías y *ḥuṣūn*," 142, and especially, 165–6.
14 Curta, "Markets," 305–6n3; Francisco Franco-Sánchez, "The Andalusian Economy in the Times of Almanzor. Administrative Theory and Economic Reality through Juridical and Geographic Sources," 98–101.
15 Constable, *Trade and Traders*, 113–14.
16 Ibid., 10–11; Glick, *Islamic and Christian Spain*, 138–9.
17 Constable, *Trade and Traders*, 32, 242–7; Manuel Castells, ed., *The Network Society: A Cross-Cultural Perspective*, 3–7; and, Manuel Castells, *The Internet Galaxy: Reflections on the Internet, Business, and Society*, 1–2.
18 Constable, *Trade and Traders*, 113; Abraham L. Udovitch, "Theory and Practice of Islamic Law: Some Evidence from the Geniza," 290. Janina M. Safran does not address commerce directly in her recent book, though she argues that Islamic jurists repeatedly crafted law in dialogue with other faith communities, rather than in an effort to shun or oppress them, thus demonstrating greater breadth in non-modern jurisprudence than often presumed, *Defining Boundaries in al-Andalus: Muslims, Christians, and Jews in Islamic Iberia*.
19 Goldberg, *Trade and Institutions*, 150–3.
20 Constable, *Trade and Traders*, 131.
21 Abraham L. Udovitch, "Commercial Techniques in Early Medieval Islamic Trade," 38; Constable, *Trade and Traders*, 112–37, 243.
22 Constable, *Trade and Traders*, 113–14.
23 Ibid., 122–5.
24 Ibid., 112–37.

25 Ibid., 137. Goitein concluded similarly about the role of government in Fāṭimīd Egypt (969–1171), as demonstrated by the Geniza documents. Furthermore, he maintained that although they were active in early medieval commerce, the Fāṭimīds had neither the will nor the ability to exert absolute control over economic matters, *Mediterranean Society*, vol. 1, 266–72. However, Goldberg demonstrates some government command in the prevention of nefarious embezzlement and fraud, largely through the availability of public records and information, in *Trade and Institutions*, chapter 5, especially 169.

26 Glick, *Islamic and Christian Spain*, 130.

27 Ray A. Kea, "Expansions and Contractions: World-Historical Change and the Western Sudan World-System (1200/1000 BC–1200/1250 AD)," 724.

28 Isichei, *History of African Societies*, 178.

29 Austen, *African Economic History*, 36.

30 Constable, *Trade and Traders*, 199–202. It is unclear whether Constable considers Andalusi traders "Mediterranean," and whether a "Berber" would have been understood as "Andalusi" and perhaps "Mediterranean." Other sources clearly identify "Islamic merchants" working and trading in West African towns, although they do not provide data on their ethnic identification, in Sam Nixon, Thilo Rehren, Maria Filomena Guerra, "New Light on the Early West African Gold Trade: Coin Moulds from Tadmekka, Mali," 1363.

31 Michael Brett and Werner Forman, *The Moors: Islam and the West*, 29; Glick, *Islamic and Christian Spain*, 132. *Al-murabiṭūn* means "the Almoravids" and derives from *ribāṭ*, which signifies "fortresses." *Al-murabiṭūn* are the men of the fortress, Brett and Forman, *Moors*, 27.

32 *Corpus of Early Arabic Sources for West African History*, 85; Nixon, Rehren, and Guerra, "New Light," 1356–7, 1365.

33 Constable, *Trade and Traders*, 202–3; Glick, *Islamic and Christian Spain*, 130–1.

34 Constable, *Trade and Traders*, 50; Glick, *Islamic and Christian Spain*, 135, 363.

35 Joseph J. Duggan, *The* Cantar de mio Cid*: Poetic Creation in Its Economic and Social Contexts*, 18.

36 Duggan, *Cantar*, 146–7.

37 In a recent study of the port city of Aden in the Indian Ocean system, Roxani Eleni Margariti contends that the interests and ambitions of individuals involved in shipping and trade sometimes produced "regional tensions and personal conflicts," in *Aden and the Indian Ocean Trade: 150 Years in the Life of a Medieval Arabian Port*, 26, 91, 125–6. In contrast to Margariti's assessment, which may constitute a difference of focus rather than diverging conclusions, Lakshmi Subramanian asserts that Hindu

and Muslim traders formed a syncretic, common tradition of religion and faith that superseded other kinds of differences, including religion, *Medieval Seafarers of India*, 34–7. Goldberg raises a number of objections to conventional approaches to commercial partnerships and trade in the Geniza documents, questioning in particular the notion that merchants trafficked and operated largely without constraint. Instead, she argues that law and government restricted their activities more than previously thought, in *Trade and Institutions*, 17 and passim.

38 Constable, *Trade and Traders*, 59–60. Contrast the open trading of the Andalusi and Cairo Geniza milieus to recent analysis of the thirteenth-century documents from the port of Quseir on the Red Sea, which indicates trade exclusively within the Muslim community, and not with Christians and Jews, Li Guo, *Commerce, Culture, and Community in a Red Sea Port*. The temporal gap between the Cairo Geniza and Quseir manuscripts may account for the discrepancy in the communities served.

39 Abraham L. Udovitch, *Partnership and Profit in Medieval Islam*, 250.

40 Constable, *Trade and Traders*, 57–65.

41 Goitein, *Mediterranean Society*, vol. 1, 149–53.

42 Constable, *Trade and Traders*, 68.

43 Goitein, *Mediterranean Society*, vol. 1, 87, 153–64. Constable demonstrated that cooperation and partnership were indistinguishable in medieval trade, *Trade and Traders*, 67. Goitein and Mordechai Akiva Friedman concur about the ubiquitous partnerships among merchants in the medieval Mediterranean, in *India Traders of the Middle Ages: Documents from the Cairo Geniza ("India Book")*, 62.

44 Goitein and Friedman, *India Traders*, 62.

45 Constable, *Trade and Traders*, 67–8.

46 Greif contends that the Jewish traders of the Cairo Geniza did not use a system of hierarchy and authority, but "a set of cultural rules of behavior – merchants' law" that directed agents on procedure, should something occur outside the purview of the merchant's instructions, *Institutions*, 70.

47 Goitein, *Mediterranean Society*, vol. 1, 169.

48 Greif, *Institutions*, 285.

49 Ibid., 61, 278–82.

50 Ibid., 284–5.

51 Ibid., 61–2; Goitein, *Mediterranean Society*, vol. 1, 166.

52 Greif, *Institutions*, 63–8. Scholars have recently challenged some of these views, including Edwards and Ogilvie, "Contract Enforcement," 438–41; Goldberg, *Trade and Institutions*, 12–14, 148–64.

53 Constable, *Trade and Traders*, 70–2; Goitein, *Mediterranean Society*, vol. 1, 169–71; Goldberg, *Traders and Institutions*, 125. Perhaps the discrepancy about the *qirāḍ* contract is due to whether or not the traders involved were concerned with satisfying the demands of either Jewish or Muslim law, or both.
54 Goitein, *Mediterranean Society*, vol. 1, 173, 442n14; Constable, *Trade and Traders*, 70–1.
55 Goldberg, *Trade and Institutions*, 82–3.
56 Constable, *Trade and Traders*, 76.
57 Ibid., 77.
58 Constable, *Trade and Traders*, 241–2.
59 Goldberg, *Trade and Institutions*, 319
60 Ibid., 315, 319–22.
61 Constable, *Trade and Traders*, 241–7.
62 Ibid., 256.
63 Ross E. Dunn, *The Adventures of Ibn Battuta: A Muslim Traveler of the Fourteenth Century*, 17.
64 Ibid., 15–16.
65 Brett and Forman, *Moors*, 36–7.
66 Constable, *Trade and Traders*, 249.
67 Anthony Pagden, *Lords of All the World: Ideologies of Empire in Spain*, 64. Pagden evidently does not consider economic prosperity a sign of medieval opportunity for glory and social advancement, despite the affluence of merchants such as Abraham Ben Yijū, S.D. Goitein, *Letters of Medieval Jewish Traders*, 12, 186, 202. Additionally, the Geniza documents contain many examples of social mobility, rather than a rigid caste system, Goitein, *Mediterranean Society*, vol. 1, 79.

4 Non-modern Iberian Travel and the Islamicate Travel Network

1 Thomas F. Glick, *Islamic and Christian Spain in the Early Middle Ages*, 13.
2 S.D. Goitein, *A Mediterranean Society: The Jewish Communities of the Arab World as Portrayed in the Documents of the Cairo Geniza*, vol. 1, 347. Olivia Remie Constable argued that non-Muslims routinely obtained certificates of safe conduct when travelling in the Islamicate commercial network, *Trade and Traders in Muslim Spain: The Commercial Realignment of the Iberian Peninsula, 900–1500*, 64.
3 Methal R. Mohammad-Marzouk, "Knowledge, Culture, and Positionality: Analysis of Three Medieval Muslim Travel Accounts," 8.
4 Elizabeth Isichei, *A History of African Societies to 1870*, 175.

5 The Kharijites were dissident followers of Islam who rejected the authority of the caliphs first in Damascus and then in Baghdad as inheritors of Muhammad's "theocratic rule," in Ralph A. Austen, *Trans-Saharan Africa in World History*, 21.
6 Ibid., 23–6.
7 María Jesús Viguera Molins, "Al-Andalus y oriente: crónica de una historia compartida," 38–41; Dimitri Gutas, *Greek Thought, Arabic Culture: The Graeco-Arabic Translation Movement in Baghdad and Early 'Abbasid Society (2nd–4th/8th–10th Centuries)*, 156–7. Al-Mansūr of Baghdad (ruled 754–75) initiated 'Abbāsid translation projects, which continued with his successor al-Mahdī (775–85). Numerous scholars attest to centuries of exchange with the east, including Michael Brett and Werner Forman, *The Moors: Islam in the West*; Isichei, *History of African Societies*, 172–95; L.P. Harvey, *Islamic Spain, 1250–1500*; and, Constable, *Trade and Traders*.
8 *Corpus of Early Arabic Sources for West African History*, 306–8.
9 *Al-Ghazal y la embajada hispano-musulmana a los vikingos en el siglo IX*.
10 A.J. Wensinck and B. Lewis, "Hadjdj."
11 Ch. Pellat, "Ibn Ḏjubayr, Abu 'l-Ḥusayn Muḥammad b. Aḥmad b. Ḏjubayr al-Kinānī."
12 Viguera Molins, "Al-Andalus y oriente," 36.
13 Dominique Urvoy, "Effets pervers du *ḥajj*, d'après le cas d'al-Andalus": "Parfois même, il ne s'agit pas seulement de montrer que l'Espagne a fait aussi bien que l'Orient; l'auteur veut montrer qu'elle a fait mieux," 44.
14 Ian Richard Netton, "Preface," in *Golden Roads: Migration, Pilgrimage, and Travel in Medieval and Modern Islam*, xiii.
15 Urvoy, "Effets pervers du *ḥajj*," 46–7.
16 Sam I. Gellens, "The Search for Knowledge in Medieval Muslim Societies: A Comparative Approach," 56; Houari Touati, *Islam and Travel in the Middle Ages*, 2; Viguera Molins, "Al-Andalus y oriente," 36.
17 Glick, *Islamic and Christian Spain*, 357.
18 Juan Vernet, *Historia de la ciencia española*, 66.
19 Gellens, "Search for Knowledge," 59.
20 Juan Vernet, "La ciencia en el Islam y Occidente," 543.
21 Gellens, "Search for Knowledge," 62.
22 The Geniza documents emphasize the importance of the travelling companion called the *rafīq*, and admonish those who let their friends or loved ones travel alone, in Goitein, *Mediterranean Society*, vol. 1, 347–8; Norbert Ohler, *The Medieval Traveller*, x.
23 S.D. Goitein, *Jews and Arabs: Their Contacts Through the Ages*, 188.
24 Diana Webb, *Medieval European Pilgrimage, c. 700–c. 1500*, 5.

25 Abderrahman El Moudden, "The Ambivalence of *Riḥla*: Community Integration and Self-Definition in Moroccan Travel Accounts," 70.
26 Sylvia Chiffoleau and Anna Madoeuf, *Les pèlerinages au Maghreb et au Moyen-Orient: espaces publics, espaces du public*, 10.
27 Webb, *Medieval European Pilgrimage*, 3.
28 Francisco Márquez Villanueva, *Santiago: trayectoria de un mito*, 104.
29 Márquez Villanueva, *Santiago*, 100, 112–13; Luis Vázquez de Parga, José María Lacarra, and Juan Uría Ríu, *Las peregrinaciones a Santiago de Compostela*, vol. 1, 53–4; Webb, *Medieval European Pilgrimage*, 23.
30 Márquez Villanueva, *Santiago*, 111, 119–20. Early studies of architectural contributions include Emile Mâle, *Art religieux du XIIe siècle en France: étude sur les origines de l'iconographie du Moyen Age*, and Manuela Churruca, *Influjo oriental en los temas iconográficos de la miniatura española, siglos X al XII*.
31 Glick discusses the role of Jews in *Islamic and Christian Spain*, 358. Cyrille Aillet demonstrates that "Mozarab" has a complicated meaning and has been used in various ways, though it never designated a unified Christian community, "Introducción," in *¿Existe una identidad mozárabe? Historia, lengua y cultura de los cristianos de al-Andalus (siglos IX–XII)*, xi.
32 Glick, *Islamic and Christian Spain*, 362.
33 Cyrille Aillet, *Les mozarabes. Christianisme, islamisation et arabization en peninsula ibérique (IXe–XIIe siècle)*, 34.
34 Márquez Villanueva, *Santiago*, 79–83.
35 José Luis Barreiro Rivas, *La función política de los caminos de peregrinación en la Europa medieval: estudio del Camino de Santiago*, 17, 111. Chiffoleau and Madoeuf agree that pilgrimages contributed to the design of itineraries that reinforced the coherence of sacred geography ("À l'échelle régionale, on a vu à quel point les pèlerinages contribuent à dessiner des itinéraires qui renforcent la cohérence de la géographie sacrée"), in *Les pèlerinages au Maghreb et au Moyen-Orient*, 14.
36 Jean Dangler, "The Idea of *Convivencia* in the Era of Hispanic Expansion: Parallel Routes in Iberia and the Maghreb," 141–61.
37 Thomas D. Spaccarelli, *A Medieval Pilgrim's Companion: Reassessing* El libro de los huéspedes *(Escorial MS. h.I.13)*, 31.
38 Ohler, *Medieval Traveller*, 80–5.
39 Jonathan Sumption, *The Age of Pilgrimage: The Medieval Journey to God*, 284.
40 Ibid., 289; Ohler, *Medieval Traveller*, 89–96.
41 Ross E. Dunn, *The Adventures of Ibn Battuta: A Muslim Traveler of the Fourteenth Century*, 11; Marshall G.S. Hodgson, "The Role of Islam in World History," 113–16.

42 Glick, *Islamic and Christian*, 13–14.
43 Constable, *Trade and Traders*, 59–60.
44 Olivia Remie Constable, *Housing the Stranger in the Mediterranean World: Lodging, Trade, and Travel in Late Antiquity and the Middle Ages*, 2.
45 Ibid., 5–9.

5 Feudalism, "Slavery," and Poverty

1 Thomas F. Glick, *Islamic and Christian Spain in the Early Middle Ages*, 241–2; Abilio Barbero and Marcelo Vigil, *La formación del feudalismo en la Península Ibérica*.
2 Glick, *Islamic and Christian Spain*, 179, 220–1.
3 Ibid., xvii, 226–7, 244. In partial opposition to Glick, Eduardo Manzano Moreno rejects the tribalism of early Muslim conquerors and argues instead that soldiers and armies directed by the Caliphate in Damascus settled in the peninsula by way of pacts and compromises with Visigothic elites, "Prólogo a esta edición," xvii.
4 Marshall G.S. Hodgson, "The Role of Islam in World History," 15–16.
5 Glick, *Islamic and Christian Spain*, 156; Marc Bloch, *La sociétè féodale: la formation des liens de dépendence*, 221. Adam J. Kosto recently assessed how historians treated Iberia in debates on European feudalism, in "What about Spain? Iberia in the Historiography of Medieval European Feudalism," 135–58. Unfortunately, however, he fails to note Glick's discussions in *Islamic and Christian Spain*.
6 Glick, *Islamic and Christian Spain*, 86–7, 241–2; Barbero and Vigil, *La formación del feudalismo*, 354–7, 384, 394.
7 Glick, *Islamic and Christian Spain*, xvi–xvii.
8 Ibid., 241.
9 Ibid., 241; Thomas F. Glick, *From Muslim Fortress to Christian Castle: Social and Cultural Change in Medieval Spain*, 90–1, 115–16.
10 Glick notes that even the subsequent control of mills by lay lords and ecclesiastical officials in northern Iberia did not lead to "seigniorial monopoly," in *Islamic and Christian Spain*, 161.
11 Glick, *From Muslim Fortress*, chapter 4, especially 69–70, and chapter 5, 117–18.
12 Glick, *Islamic and Christian Spain*, 151–2.
13 Ibid., 153–4.
14 Ibid., 154.
15 Dolores Oliver Pérez, *El 'Cantar de mío Cid': génesis y autoría*, 16–17.
16 Glick, *Islamic and Christian Spain*, 153.

17 D. Fairchild Ruggles, "The Geographic and Social Mobility of Slaves: The Rise of Shajar al'Durr, A Slave-Concubine in Thirteenth-Century Egypt," 42.

18 S.D. Goitein, *A Mediterranean Society: The Jewish Communities of the Arab World as Portrayed in the Documents of the Cairo Geniza*, vol. 1, 132, 147, and passim; S.D. Goitein, *Jews and Arabs: Their Contacts Through the Ages*, 28, 102.

19 *Corpus of Early Arabic Sources for West African History*, 479. Moses I. Finley claimed that Anglo-American anthropologists subsume a variety of African workers under the rubric of "slave," rather than devising more accurate names for different kinds of laborers, *Ancient Slavery and Modern Ideology*, 137–8.

20 *Corpus*, 13, 18, 68, and passim.

21 Goitein, *Mediterranean Society*, vol. 1, 147; John Docker, *1492: The Poetics of Diaspora*, 11.

22 Leslie Peirce, "An Imperial Caste: Inverted Racialization in the Architecture of Ottoman Sovereignty," 30.

23 S.D. Goitein and Mordechai Akiva Friedman, *India Traders of the Middle Ages: Documents from the Cairo Geniza ("India Book")*, 52–89, especially 66; and, S.D. Goitein, *Letters of Medieval Jewish Traders*, 13, 186, 191n18.

24 Olivia Remie Constable, *Trade and Traders in Muslim Spain: The Commercial Realignment of the Iberian Peninsula, 900–1500*, 203–4.

25 Ibn Ḥazm al-Andalusī, *El collar de la paloma (Ṭawq al-Ḥamāma)*, 92–3; D. Fairchild Ruggles, "Mothers of a Hybrid Dynasty: Race, Genealogy, and Acculturation in al-Andalus," especially 69–77.

26 Peirce, "Imperial Caste," 28–9; Ruggles, "Mothers of a Hybrid Dynasty," 71.

27 Manuela Marín, *Al-Andalus y los andalusíes*, 44–6.

28 Zidane Zéraoui and Roberto Marín Guzmán, *Árabes y musulmanes en Europa: historia y procesos migratorios*, 130–2; Goitein, *Mediterranean Society*, vol. 1, 400n5.

29 Marín, *Al-Ándalus*, 46; Manuela Marín, *Individuo y sociedad en al-Ándalus*, 41–6; Ahmad Mukhtār 'Abd al-Fattāh al-Abbādī, *Los eslavos en España: ojeada sobre su origen, desarrollo y relación con el movimiento de la Su'ūbiyya*, 24–6.

30 Goitein, *Mediterranean Society*, vol. 1, 131. Elizabeth Isichei cites the Tyeddo of Senegal, a group of "slave soldiers" who formed an aristocracy, *A History of African Societies to 1870*, 94–5. Scholars cite a long history of military "slavery" in the Islamicate world, as in the case of the renowned Mamlūks, which literally means "things possessed" in Arabic, a group of "slave" soldiers who ruled Egypt and Syria from 1250 to 1517, D. Ayalon, "Mamlūk," and D. Sourdel, "Ghulām."

31 Constable, *Trade and Traders*, 205–6.

32 Ibid., 206.

33 Isichei, *History of African Societies*, 94–5, 178; Ralph A. Austen, *African Economic History: Internal Development and External Dependency*, 36.

34 Isichei underscores the difference in noting that the growth of Atlantic and Saharan slave trafficking constituted a new mode of production, *History of African Societies*, 94.

35 William D. Phillips, Jr, *Slavery in Medieval and Early Modern Iberia*, 10–14.

36 Mark R. Cohen, *Poverty and Charity in the Jewish Community of Medieval Egypt*, 1, 4; and Michel Mollat, *The Poor in the Middle Ages: An Essay in Social History*, 2, 5.

37 Cohen, *Poverty and Charity*, 4–5; Mollat, *Poor in the Middle Ages*, 9.

38 Cohen, *Poverty and Charity*, 7.

39 Ibid., 69.

40 Goitein, *Mediterranean Society*, vol. 1, 98.

41 Ibid., 98; Goitein, *Mediterranean Society*, vol. 5, 73–94; and Mark R. Cohen, *The Voice of the Poor in the Middle Ages: An Anthology of Documents from the Cairo Geniza*.

42 Glick, *Islamic and Christian Spain*, 113.

43 Teófilo Ruiz, *From Heaven to Earth: The Reordering of Castilian Society, 1150–1350*, 116.

44 Glick, *Islamic and Christian Spain*, 159–66.

45 Ibid., 166–9.

46 Ibid., 120.

47 Ruiz, *From Heaven to Earth*, 116.

48 Ibid., 129.

49 Ramzi Rouighi, *The Making of a Mediterranean Emirate: Ifrīqiyā and Its Andalusis, 1200–1400*, 57–8.

6 Politics

1 Ray A. Kea, ""Expansions and Contractions: World-Historical Change and the Western Sudan World-System (1200/1000 BC–1200/1250 AD)," 726.

2 Thomas F. Glick, *Islamic and Christian Spain in the Early Middle Ages*, 363.

3 Eduardo Manzano Moreno, "Christian-Muslim Frontier in Al-Andalus: Idea and Reality," 86, 90–1.

4 Ibn al-Kardabūs, *Historia de al-Andalus (Kitāb al-Iktifā')*, 98–100. Little is known about the life of the historiographer Ibn al-Kardabūs. Although he was probably of Andalusi origin, since his lineage or *nisba* suggests Cordova, during the second half of the twelfth century he resided in

Tozeur in southern Tunisia and died in the early thirteenth century, 13–14.

5 Hugh Kennedy, *Muslim Spain and Portugal: A Political History of Al-Andalus*, xiv.

6 Michael Brett and Werner Forman, *The Moors: Islam in the West*, 29.

7 Peter Linehan, "At the Spanish Frontier," 46, 50.

8 Elena Lourie, "The Will of Alfonso I, 'El Batallador,' King of Aragon and Navarre: A Reassessment," 635–51.

9 Ron Barkai, *Cristianos y musulmanes en la España medieval. El enemigo en el espejo*, 147.

10 For examples of Alfonso's descriptions of Muslims in his historiography, see chapters 554 through 559 of the *Estoria de Espanna* (*Prosa histórica*, 89–100), which include the story of the weakness of the last Visigothic king, Rodrigo, in allowing the Muslims access to the peninsula. In this case, Alfonso points to Rodrigo's inadequacies rather than expressing antagonism or hatred toward the North Africans.

For a contrasting view, however, see the *General Estoria*, part I, book II, chapter 29 (*The Electronic Texts and Concordance of the Prose Works of Alfonso X*, GE1, fol. 21v), where Alfonso's scribe narrates the biblical story about Christian and Muslim difference, in which Christians derived from Japhet, and Muslims from Cham. As the initial rubric indicates, the writer intends to show that Christians and Muslims were enemies because of their divergent origins ({RUB. Donde uino la p<r>i'ncipal enemistad d<e>los fijos de Japhet & d<e>los de Ca<m>.}). Although the scribe claims that Christians do not err in capturing and enslaving Muslims, the extent to which Alfonso converted this disparaging sentiment into a fervent military or political campaign against thirteenth-century Andalusis is yet to be confirmed. The scribe's recounting of the biblical story may be, at least in part, formulaic.

11 Anthony Pym, *Negotiating the Frontier: Translators and Intercultures in Hispanic History*, 140.

12 Leonardo Funes, *El modelo historiográfico alfonsí: una caracterización*, 9.

13 Linehan, "At the Spanish Frontier," 39, 52.

14 Funes, *Modelo historiográfico*, 9–10: " … con la colaboración del círculo intelectual más numeroso y erudito de su época en el Occidente europeo, integrado por cristianos, judíos y musulmanes … "

15 Robert Ignatius Burns, SJ, *Medieval Colonialism: Postcrusade Exploitation of Islamic Valencia*, 9, 11.

16 Fernando García de Cortázar and José Manuel González Vesga, *Breve historia de España*, 136. Glick notes that a Goth military elite

of approximately 200,000 governed an Iberian ("Hispano-Roman") population of approximately seven million, *Islamic and Christian Spain*, 14.

17 García de Cortázar and González Vesga, *Breve historia*, 152, 156: "Como en los tiempos godos, el afianzamiento del emirato dependía de la puesta en pie de una eficaz estructura política, que, al margen de la diversidad, terminara por integrarla y facilitara su control," 156 [As occurred during the Gothic era, the emirate's strengthening depended on the creation of an effective political structure, which despite its inherent diversity, would end up integrating and facilitating its control]; Glick, *Islamic and Christian Spain*, 5–10.

18 Ralph W. Brauer, *Boundaries and Frontiers in Medieval Muslim Geography*, 13, and 26–7. R.S. O'Fahey demonstrates a similar, historical understanding of the Islamic frontier of Sūdān as a sphere of influence and a state of mind, "Fūr and Fartīt: The History of a Frontier," 85.

19 Albert Habib Hourani, *A History of the Arabic Peoples*, 138.

20 Ross E. Dunn, *The Adventures of Ibn Battuta: A Muslim Traveler of the Fourteenth Century*, 11.

21 Glick, *Islamic and Christian Spain*, 13–14.

22 José Antonio Maravall, *El concepto de España en la Edad Media*, 369–71.

23 Ibid., 371, 376–9, 388–9.

24 Glick, *Islamic and Christian Spain*, 238–9.

25 Eduardo Manzano Moreno, *Historia de España: épocas medievales*, vol. 2, especially 263–8.

26 Glick, *Islamic and Christian Spain*, 225–6.

27 Ibid., 239.

28 John Watts, *The Making of Polities: Europe, 1300–1500*, especially 34–5.

29 Ibid., especially 13–30.

30 Ibid., 39–41.

31 Glick, *Islamic and Christian Spain*, 239.

32 Emilio Mitre Fernández, "La cristiandad medieval y las formulaciones fronterizas," 40–7, 51.

33 Teófilo F. Ruiz, *From Heaven to Earth: The Reordering of Castilian Society, 1150–1350*, 84.

34 Mitre Fernández, "Cristiandad medieval," 47.

35 Ruiz, *Heaven to Earth*, 68.

36 Ibid., 68, 72. A modern *mojón* divides Spain and France in Llívia, the Catalan and Spanish enclave bordered by France, "Llívia," Wikipedia, http://es.wikipedia.org/wiki/Llivia.

37 Glick, *Islamic and Christian Spain*, 106.

38 Ruiz, *Heaven to Earth*, 73. We discussed the incipient rise of this sociopolitical and geographical stratification in our discussion of feudalism in chapter 5.
39 Ibid., 77.
40 Ibid., 82–3.
41 María Asenjo González, "Actividad económica, aduanas y relaciones de poder en la frontera norte de Castilla en el reinado de los Reyes Católicos," 277. A *portazgo* is a medieval tax much like a toll (*peaje*) for passage between zones. It may refer to the use of a pass by a transhumant shepherd and his or her livestock, although Constable contends that it constitutes a tariff list attached to an urban charter, *Trade and Traders*, 46.
42 Miguel Ángel Ladero Quesada, "Sobre la evolución de las fronteras medievales hispánicas (siglos XI a XIV)," 42.
43 Asenjo González, "Actividad económica," 308–9.
44 Ladero Quesada, "Sobre la evolución," 47.
45 Ruiz, *Heaven to Earth*, 84.
46 Isabel Montes Romero-Camacho, "El comercio exterior de cereales en el Reino de Sevilla durante el siglo XV," 111.
47 José Antonio Maravall, *Estado moderno y mentalidad social (siglos XV a XVII)*, vol. 1, 130–1; Mitre Fernández, *Fronteras y fronterizos*, 42–4.
48 Maravall, *Estado moderno*, 131.
49 Robert Bartlett notes attempts toward homogeneity in late medieval and early modern Iberia as well in the shift from the "personality" to the "territoriality" of the law from the twelfth through the sixteenth centuries, that is, from "pluralism to uniformity," which was evident in 1290 when the Castilian king Sancho IV decried the uneven treatment of Mozarabs and Castilians, since they should all receive equal or uniform treatment under the law, *The Making of Europe: Conquest, Colonization, and Cultural Change, 950–1350*, 220.

7 Identity and Culture

1 Alberto Montaner Frutos, "*Cantar de mio Cid*," in *Dictionary of Literary Biography*, vol. 337, 29.
2 *Bando* was the term most applied to the Cid's antagonists, Michael Harney, *Kinship and Polity in the* Poema de mío Cid, 73–4.
3 Michael Brett and Werner Forman, *The Moors: Islam in the West*, 26.
4 Thomas F. Glick, *Islamic and Christian Spain in the Early Middle Ages*, 182; Ramón Menéndez Pidal, *La España del Cid*, vol. 1, 31, 170, 176–8, 279–85.

5 As we discussed, "Mozarab" is a variable, complex term that never signified a united Christian community, Cyrille Aillet, "Introducción," in *¿Existe una identidad mozárabe? Historia, lengua y cultura de los cristianos de al-Andalus (siglos IX–XII)*, xi; Cyrille Aillet, *Les mozarabes. Christianisme, islamisation et arabization en peninsula ibérique (IXe –XIIe siècle)*, 34.
6 Tabish Khair, "African and Asian Travel Texts in the Light of Europe: An Introduction," 18; and, *Other Routes: 1500 Years of African and Asian Travel Writing*, 54.
7 Jacqueline Sublet, "Nisba."
8 Sublet, "Nisba"; Elizabeth Isichei, *A History of African Societies to 1870*, 94–5.
9 Manuela Marín, *Al-Ándalus y los andalusíes*, 29, 33–4.
10 Glick, *Islamic and Christian Spain*, 154.
11 Harney, *Kinship and Polity*, 14, 77–8.
12 Manuel Tuñón de Lara, *Historia de España*, vol. 1, 133.
13 José Ángel García Cortázar and José Manuel González Vesga, *Breve historia de España*, 78–84.
14 Olivia Remie Constable, *Trade and Traders in Muslim Spain: The Commercial Realignment of the Iberian Peninsula, 900–1500*, 57; María Rosa Menocal, *The Ornament of the World: How Muslims, Jews, and Christians Created a Culture of Tolerance in Medieval Spain*, 86–7.

Brent Nongbri analyses religion as a modern phenomenon, which is understood as a private, idealized, and interior realm. He shows that the Latin *religio*, the Greek *thrēskeia*, and the Arabic *dīn*, all of which are translated today as "religion," connoted notions and domains including the social order, law, ethics, and morality, which fall outside the modern scope of religious belief and practice. Not only did "religion" signify differently in non-modern periods, but it also failed to serve as a universal rationale for political and cultural association, as we saw in the diverse interfaith political alliances in chapter 6. Brent Nongbri, *Before Religion: A History of a Modern Concept*, 26–45.
15 Constable, *Trade and Traders*, 57–9. Constable did not speculate about what "ethnic" might have meant in the non-modern world, even though scholars usually consider ethnicity a modern category and mode of identification.
16 Jeremy Edwards and Sheilagh Ogilvie, "Contract Enforcement, Institutions, and Social Capital: The Maghribi Traders Reappraised," 12. Many of the merchants' letters in the Geniza collection were written in the Arabic dialect of the Jewish community at Fusṭāṭ, though in Hebrew script, a form now called Judeo-Arabic, Jessica L. Goldberg, *Trade and Institutions*

in the Medieval Mediterranean: The Geniza Merchants and Their Business World, 7.

17 Edwards and Ogilvie, "Contract Enforcement," 12.

18 Manuel Ruzafa García, "Valencia, puerto mediterráneo y atlántico en el s. XV. Relaciones con Andalucía, reino de Granada y norte de África," 98–9. Curiously, Goldberg argues that the Geniza documents do not indicate strict correspondence between merchants' business activities and "geographies of religious communities or family connections," citing the case of an Andalusi merchant with family ties in Madrid and Toledo, who seemed to reside and conduct business only in Egypt and the Levant, also called al-Shām, in *Trade and Institutions*, 25.

19 Olivia Remie Constable, *Housing the Stranger in the Mediterranean World: Lodging, Trade, and Travel in Late Antiquity and the Middle Ages*, 117.

20 Olivia Remie Constable, "*Fondaco*," 195.

21 Constable, *Housing the Stranger*, 116–17; Robert Bartlett, *The Making of Europe: Conquest, Colonization, and Cultural Change, 950–1350*, 197–204; Khair, "African and Asian Travel," 4; Patrick J. Geary, *Myth of Nations: The Medieval Origins of Europe*, 40, 55.

22 Isichei, *History of African Societies*, 124, 175.

23 José Antonio Maravall, *El concepto de España en la Edad Media*, 371–2, 387.

24 Glick, *Islamic and Christian Spain*, 363; Eduardo Manzano Moreno, *Historia de España: épocas medievales*, vol. 2, 340–2. Manzano Moreno notes Cluny's lack of influence in Aragon and Catalunya, 342.

25 Glick, *Islamic and Christian Spain*, 363; Manzano Moreno, *Historia de España*, 342–4.

26 Maribel Fierro, "Alfonso X 'The Wise': The Last Almohad Caliph?," 194.

27 Francisco Márquez Villanueva offered many important links between Andalusi and Arab cultural and intellectual production, and Alfonso's project, in *El concepto cultural alfonsí*.

28 Cynthia Robinson, *In Praise of Song: The Making of Courtly Culture in al-Andalus and Provence, 1005–1134 AD*, 19. Glick argues similarly, contending that with the exception of Catalunya, an urban economy in early medieval "Christian" realms meant an "Islamic" way of life, since the Islamicate model was "proximate, overarching, and compelling," *Islamic and Christian Spain*, 116.

29 Rosa María Rodríguez Porto, "Courtliness and Its *Trujamanes*: Manufacturing Chivalric Imagery across the Castilian-Grenadine Frontier."

30 Sylvia Chiffoleau and Anna Madoeuf, *Les pèlerinages au Maghreb et au Moyen-Orient: espaces publics, espaces du public*, 10.

31 José Luis Barreiro Rivas, *La función política de los caminos de peregrinación en la Europa medieval: estudio del Camino de Santiago*: "Es el *espacio emergente* donde cobran plena importancia las acciones orientadas a la creación de identidades colectivas y de vínculos simbólicos entre los súbditos y el poder," 279.

32 M.E. McMillan, *The Meaning of Mecca: The Politics of Pilgrimage in Early Islam*, 27.

33 Dominique Urvoy, "Effets pervers du hajj, d'après le cas d'al-Andalus," 44, 46–7; Ian Richard Netton, "Preface," in *Golden Roads: Migration, Pilgrimage, and Travel in Medieval and Modern Islam*, xiii.

34 Francisco Márquez Villanueva, *Santiago: trayectoria de un mito*, 79–83, 112–13; Barreiro Rivas, *Función política de los caminos de peregrinación*, 283–91, 307.

35 Peter Brown, *The Cult of the Saints: Its Rise and Function in Latin Christianity*, 8–11.

36 It is interesting to contrast political uses of pilgrimage to travel for knowledge in the Islamicate network, *riḥla* and *ṭalab al-'ilm*, which served to instill a feeling of local identity and pride among Andalusi Muslims, rather than a sense of marginalization from eastern intellectual centres. The journeys became even more important for linking Andalusi Muslims to the larger *umma* after the fall of Toledo in 1085 and the subsequent strengthening of Hispanicate kingdoms, Sam I. Gellens, "The Search for Knowledge in Medieval Muslim Societies: A Comparative Approach," 56, 60–1.

37 Jean Dangler, "The Idea of *Convivencia* in the Era of Hispanic Expansion: Parallel Routes in Iberia and the Maghreb."

38 Barreiro Rivas, *Función política de los caminos de peregrinación*, 36.

39 Glick, *Islamic and Christian Spain*, 362.

40 Márquez Villanueva, *Santiago*, 79–83.

Epilogue

1 María Rosa Menocal, *The Arabic Role in Medieval Literary History: A Forgotten Heritage*, 103; María Rosa Menocal, *Shards of Love: Exile and the Origins of the Lyric*, 154–83; see my discussion in *Making Difference in Medieval and Early Modern Iberia*, 57–8; David A. Wacks, *Framing Iberia:* Maqāmāt *and Frametale Narratives in Medieval Spain*.

2 G. Schoeler and W. Stoetzer, "Zadjal."

3 Menocal, *Arabic Role*; Josiah Blackmore and Gregory S. Hutcheson, *Queer Iberia: Sexualities, Cultures, and Crossings from the Middle Ages to the Renaissance*, 1–13.

4 For additional perspectives, scholars offer numerous ways to reframe cultural studies in the recent cluster in *PMLA*, "Reframing Postcolonial and Global Studies in the Longer *Durée*."

5 Mónica Bolufer and Montserrat Cabré survey the gender debates in Spain from a perspective that acknowledges the intersections between politics, cultural attitudes, and book production, though they do not apply system and network principles, in "La querelle des femmes en Espagne: bilan sur l'histoire d'un débat (1400–1800)."

6 Tony Kushner predicted as much in 1994 in an article in *The Nation*, where he warned of shortsighted goals of the gay and lesbian rights movement of the time, in "A Socialism of the Skin."

Works Cited

Abel, A. "Dār al-Ḥarb." *Encyclopedia of Islam, Second Edition*. Ed. P. Bearman, Th. Bianquis, C.E. Bosworth, E. van Donzel, and W.P. Heinrichs. Leiden: Brill Online, 2013.

– "Dār al-Islām." *Encyclopedia of Islam, Second Edition*. Ed. P. Bearman, Th. Bianquis, C.E. Bosworth, E. van Donzel, and W.P. Heinrichs. Leiden: Brill Online, 2013.

Abulafia, David. "Introduction: Seven Types of Ambiguity, c. 1100–c. 1500." *Medieval Frontiers: Concepts and Practices*. Ed. David Abulafia and Nora Berend. Burlington: Ashgate, 2002. 1–34.

Abu-Lughod, Janet L. *Before European Hegemony: The World System A.D. 1250–1350*. New York: Oxford University Press, 1989.

Acién Almansa, Manuel. "Poblamiento y sociedad en al-Andalus: un mundo de ciudades, alquerías y *ḥuṣūn*." *Cristiandad e Islam en la Edad Media hispana*. Ed. José Ignacio de la Iglesia Duarte. Logroño: Institutos de Estudios Riojanos, 2008. 141–67.

Aillet, Cyrille. "Introducción." *¿Existe una identidad mozárabe? Historia, lengua y cultura de los cristianos de al-Andalus (siglos IX–XII)*. Ed. Cyrille Aillet, Mayte Penelas, and Philippe Roisse. Madrid: Casa de Velázquez, 2008. ix–xvi.

– *Les mozarabes. Christianisme, islamisation et arabization en péninsule ibérique (IXe–XIIe siècle)*. Madrid: Casa de Velázquez, 2010.

Al-Abbādī, Ahmad Mukhtār 'Abd al-Fattāh. *Los eslavos en España: ojeada sobre su origen, desarrollo y relación con el movimiento de la Su'ūbiyya*. Madrid: Ministerio de Educación de Egipto, Instituto Egipcio de Estudios Islámicos, 1953.

Al-Ghazal y la embajada hispano-musulmana a los vikingos en el siglo IX. Ed. Mariano G. Campo. Madrid: Miraguano, 2002.

Al-Ḥimyarī, Abū 'Abd Allāh Muhammad Ibn 'Abd al-Mun'im. *Kitāb al-Rawd al-Mi'tar* (The Book of the Fragrant Gardens). Trans. María Pilar Maestro González. Valencia: [Gráficas Bautista], 1963.

Alfonso X. *General Estoria* (GE1). *On The Electronic Texts and Concordances of the Prose Works of Alfonso X, El Sabio*. Ed. Lloyd Kasten, John Nitti, and Wilhelmina Jonxis-Henkemans. Madison: Hispanic Seminary for Medieval Studies, 1997.

– *Prosa histórica*. Ed. Benito Brancaforte. Madrid: Cátedra, 1990.

Amer, Sahar, and Laura Doyle, ed. "Reframing Postcolonial and Global Studies in the Longer *Durée*." *PMLA* 130.2 (Mar. 2015): 331–438.

Anderson, Benedict. *Imagined Communities: Reflections on the Origin and Spread of Nationalism*. New York: Verso, 2006.

Asenjo González, María. "Actividad económica, aduanas y relaciones de poder en la frontera norte de Castilla en el reinado de los Reyes Católicos." *En la España medieval* 19 (1996): 275–309.

Austen, Ralph A. *African Economic History: Internal Development and External Dependency*. London: James Currey, 1987.

– *Trans-Saharan Africa in World History*. New York: Oxford University Press, 2010.

Ayalon, D. "Mamlūk." *The Encyclopedia of Islam, Second Edition*. Ed. P. Bearman, Th. Bianquis, C.E. Bosworth, E. van Donzel, and W.P. Heinrichs. Brill Online, 2016.

Balakrishnan, Gopal. "The Twilight of Capital?" *Immanuel Wallerstein and the Problem of the World: System, Scale, Culture*. Ed. David Palumbo-Liu, Bruce Robbins, and Nirvana Tanoukhi. Durham: Duke University Press, 2011. 227–32.

Barbero, Abilio, and Marcelo Vigil. *La formación del feudalismo en la Península Ibérica*. 2nd ed. Barcelona: Crítica, 2015.

Barceló, Miquel. *Arqueología medieval: en las afueras del "medievalismo."* Barcelona: Crítica, 1988.

Barkai, Ron. *Cristianos y musulmanes en la España medieval. El enemigo en el espejo*. Madrid: Rialp, 1984.

Barreiro Rivas, José Luis. *La función política de los caminos de peregrinación en la Europa medieval: estudio del Camino de Santiago*. Madrid: Tecnos, 1997.

Bartlett, Robert. *The Making of Europe: Conquest, Colonization, and Cultural Change, 950–1350*. Princeton: Princeton University Press, 1993.

Bennison, Amira K. "The Peoples of the North in the Eyes of the Muslims of Umayyad al-Andalus (711–1031)." *Journal of Global History* 2 (2007): 157–74.

Berend, Nora. "Preface." *Medieval Frontiers: Concepts and Practices*. Ed. David Abulafia and Nora Berend. Burlington: Ashgate, 2002. x–xv.

Biddick, Kathleen. "The Cut of Pedagogy: Genealogy in the Blood." *Journal of Medieval and Early Modern Studies* 30.3 (fall 2000): 449–62.

Blackmore, Josiah, and Gregory S. Hutcheson, ed. *Queer Iberia: Sexualities, Cultures, and Crossings from the Middle Ages to the Renaissance*. Durham: Duke University Press, 1999.

Bloch, Marc. *La sociétè féodale: la formation des liens de depéndance*. Paris: Albin Michel, 1939.

Bloch, R. Howard, and Stephen G. Nichols, ed. *Medievalism and the Modernist Temper*. Baltimore: Johns Hopkins University Press, 1996.

Bolufer, Mónica, and Montserrat Cabré. "La querelle des femmes en Espagne: bilan sur l'histoire d'un débat (1400–1800)." *Revisiter la querelle des femmes. Discours sur l'égalité/inégalité des femmes et des hommes à l'échelle européenne*. Ed. Marie-Elisabeth Henneau and Rotraud Von Kulessa. Saint-Étienne: Presses universitaires de Saint-Étienne, 2015. 31–67.

Braudel, Fernand. *The Mediterranean and the Mediterranean World in the Age of Phillip II*. Trans. Siân Reynolds. 2 vols. New York: Harper & Row, 1972–3.

Brauer, Ralph W. *Boundaries and Frontiers in Medieval Muslim Geography*. Vol. 85. Part 6. Philadelphia: The American Philosophical Society, 1995.

Brenner, Neil. "The Space of the World: Beyond State-Centrism?" *Immanuel Wallerstein and the Problem of the World: System, Scale, Culture*. Ed. David Palumbo-Liu, Bruce Robbins, and Nirvana Tanoukhi. Durham: Duke University Press, 2011. 101–37.

Brett, Michael, and Werner Forman. *The Moors: Islam in the West*. London: Orbis, 1980.

Brown, Catherine. "The Relics of Menéndez Pidal: Mourning and Melancholia in Hispanomedieval Studies." *La corónica* 24.1 (fall 1995): 15–41.

Brown, Peter. *The Cult of the Saints: Its Rise and Function in Latin Christianity*. Chicago: University of Chicago Press, 1981.

Brun, Javier, Director, Joaquín Benito, and Pedro Canut. *Redes culturales: claves para sobrevivir en la globalización*. Madrid: Agencia Española de Cooperación Internacional para el Desarrollo, 2008.

Burns, Robert Ignatius, SJ. *Medieval Colonialism: Postcrusade Exploitation of Islamic Valencia*. Princeton: Princeton University Press, 1975.

Butler, Judith. *Gender Trouble: Feminism and the Subversion of Identity*. New York: Routledge, 2006.

Butler, Judith, and Athena Athanasiou. *Dispossession: The Performative in the Political*. Cambridge: Polity, 2013.

Cajal, Máximo. *Ceuta, Melilla, Olivenza, Gibraltar. ¿Dónde acaba España?* Madrid: Siglo XXI, 2003.

Cantor, Norman F. *Inventing the Middle Ages: The Lives, Works, and Ideas of the Great Medievalists of the Twentieth Century*. New York: W. Morrow, 1991.

Casey, James. *Early Modern Spain: A Social History*. New York: Routledge, 1999.

Castells, Manuel. *Communication Power*. Oxford: Oxford University Press, 2009.

– "Nothing New Under the Sun?" *Connectivity in Antiquity: Globalization as Long-Term Historical Process*. Ed. Oystein S. LaBianca and Sandra Arnold Scham. London: Equinox, 2006. 158–67.

– *The Internet Galaxy: Reflections on the Internet, Business, and Society*. Oxford: Oxford University Press, 2001.

– ed. *The Network Society: A Cross-Cultural Perspective*. Cheltenham, UK, Northampton, MA: Edward Elgar, 2004.

Castro, Américo. *España en su historia: cristianos, moros y judíos*. Barcelona: Crítica, 1983.

Chalmeta, Pedro. *El zoco medieval: contribución al estudio de la historia del mercado*. Almería: Fundación Ibn Tufayl de Estudios Árabes, 2010.

Chanda, Nayan. *Bound Together: How Traders, Preachers, Adventurers, and Warriors Shaped Globalization*. New Haven: Yale University Press, 2007.

Chiffoleau, Sylvia, and Anna Madoeuf. *Les pèlerinages au Maghreb et au Moyen-Orient: espaces publics, espaces du public*. Beirut: Institut Français du Proche-Orient, 2005.

Choksy, Jamsheed K. "Zoroastrianism." *The Oxford Encyclopedia of the Islamic World*. *Oxford Islamic Studies Online*. www.oxfordislamicstudies.com/article/opr/t236/e1117

Churruca, Manuela. *Influjo oriental en los temas iconográficos de la miniatura española, siglos X al XII*. Madrid: Espasa Calpe, 1939.

Cohen, Mark R. *Poverty and Charity in the Jewish Community of Medieval Egypt*. Princeton: Princeton University Press, 2005.

– *The Voice of the Poor in the Middle Ages: An Anthology of Documents from the Cairo Geniza*. Princeton: Princeton University Press, 2005.

Constable, Olivia Remie. *Trade and Traders in Muslim Spain: The Commercial Realignment of the Iberian Peninsula, 900–1500*. Cambridge: Cambridge University Press, 1994.

– *"Fondaco." Trade, Travel, and Exploration in the Middle Ages: An Encyclopedia*. Ed. John Block Friedman and Kristen Mossler Figg. New York: Routledge, 2000. 195–6.

– "Foreword." *Medieval Trade in the Mediterranean World: Illustrative Documents*. Ed. Robert S. Lopez and Irving W. Raymond. New York: Columbia University Press, 2001. xiii–xx.

– *Housing the Stranger in the Mediterranean World: Lodging, Trade, and Travel in Late Antiquity and the Middle Ages*. New York: Cambridge University Press, 2003.

cooke, miriam, and Bruce B. Lawrence. "Introduction." *Muslim Networks: From Hajj to Hip Hop*. Ed. miriam cooke and Bruce B. Lawrence. Chapel Hill: University of North Carolina Press, 2005. 1–28.

Corpus of Early Arabic Sources for West African History. Ed. N. Levtzion and J.F.P. Hopkins. Princeton: Markus Wiener, 2000.

Curta, Florin. "Markets in Tenth-Century al-Andalus and Volga Bulghāria: Contrasting Views of Trade in Muslim Europe." *Al-Masaq*, 25.3, 2013, pp. 305–30.

Dagenâis, John. *The Ethics of Reading in Manuscript Culture: Glossing the* Libro de buen amor. Princeton: Princeton University Press, 1994.

Dangler, Jean. *Making Difference in Medieval and Early Modern Iberia*. Notre Dame: University of Notre Dame Press, 2005.

– "Edging Toward Iberia." *diacritics* 36.3–4 (fall–winter 2006): 12–26.

– "The Idea of *Convivencia* in the Era of Hispanic Expansion: Parallel Routes in Iberia and the Maghreb." *Revisiting Convivencia*. Ed. Connie Scarborough. Newark, DE: Juan de la Cuesta, 2014. 141–61.

Davis, Kathleen. *Periodization and Sovereignty: How Ideas of Feudalism and Secularization Govern the Politics of Time*. Philadelphia: University of Pennsylvania Press, 2008.

Davis, Kathleen, and Nadia Altschul. "The Idea of 'the Middle Ages' Outside Europe." *Medievalisms in the Postcolonial World: The Idea of "the Middle Ages" Outside Europe*. Ed. Kathleen Davis and Nadia Altschul. Baltimore: Johns Hopkins University Press, 2009. 1–24.

De Landa, Manuel. *A Thousand Years of Nonlinear History*. New York: Zone, 1997.

Deleuze, Gilles, and Félix Guattari. *Anti-Oedipus: Capitalism and Schizophrenia*. Minneapolis: University of Minnesota Press, 1983.

Docker, John. *1492: The Poetics of Diaspora*. New York: Continuum, 2001.

Doubleday, Simon R. "'Criminal Non-Intervention:' Hispanism, Medievalism, and the Pursuit of Neutrality." *In the Light of Medieval Spain: Islam, the West, and the Relevance of the Past*. Ed. Simon R. Doubleday and David Coleman. New York: Palgrave Macmillan, 2008. 1–31.

Duggan, Joseph J. *The* Cantar de mio Cid*: Poetic Creation in Its Economic and Social Contexts*. New York: Cambridge University Press, 1989.

Dunn, Ross E. *The Adventures of Ibn Battuta: A Muslim Traveler of the Fourteenth Century*. 2nd ed. Berkeley: University of California Press, 2005.

Dussel, Enrique D. "World-System and 'Trans'-Modernity." *Nepantla: Views from South* 3.2 (2002): 221–44.

Eco, Umberto. *Travels in Hyperreality: Essays*. Trans. William Weaver. San Diego: Harcourt Brace, 1983. 61–85.

Edwards, Jeremy, and Sheilagh Ogilvie. "Contract Enforcement, Institutions, and Social Capital: The Maghribi Traders Reappraised." *The Economic History Review* 65.2 (2012): 421–44.

Ellenblum, Ronnie. "Borders and Borderlines in the Middle Ages? The Example of the Latin Kingdom of Jerusalem." *Medieval Frontiers: Concepts and Practices*. Ed. David Abulafia and Nora Berend. Burlington: Ashgate, 2002. 105–19.

El Moudden, Abderrahman. "The Ambivalence of *Riḥla*: Community Integration and Self-Definition in Moroccan Travel Accounts." *Muslim Travellers: Pilgrimage, Migration, and the Religious Imagination*. Ed. Dale F. Eickelman and James Piscatori. New York: Routledge, 1990. 69–84.

Fierro, Maribel. "Alfonso X 'The Wise:' The Last Almohad Caliph?" *Medieval Encounters* 15 (2009): 175–98.

Finley, Moses I. *Ancient Slavery and Modern Ideology*. Ed. Brent D. Shaw. Princeton: Markus Wiener, 1998.

Franco-Sánchez, Francisco. "The Andalusian Economy in the Times of Almanzor. Administrative Theory and Economic Reality through Juridical and Geographic Sources." *Imago Temporis. Medium Aevum* 2 (2008): 83–112.

Freedman, Paul. "Spanish March." *Medieval Iberia: An Encyclopedia*. Ed. E. Michael Gerli. New York: Routledge, 2003. 761–2.

Fuchs, Barbara. "1492 and the Cleaving of Hispanism." *Journal of Medieval and Early Modern Studies* 37.3 (fall 2007): 493–510.

– *Exotic Nation: Maurophilia and the Construction of Early Modern Spain*. Philadelphia: University of Pennsylvania Press, 2009.

Funes, Leonardo. *El modelo historiográfico alfonsí: una caracterización*. London: Department of Hispanic Studies, Queen Mary and Westfield College, 1997.

García de Cortázar, Fernando, and José Manuel González Vesga. *Breve historia de España*. Madrid: Alianza, 1995.

García Fitz, Francisco. *Reconquista*. Granada: Universidad de Granada, 2010.

Geary, Patrick J. *The Myth of Nations: The Medieval Origins of Europe*. Princeton: Princeton University Press, 2002.

Gellens, Sam I. "The Search for Knowledge in Medieval Muslim Societies: A Comparative Approach." *Muslim Travellers: Pilgrimage, Migration, and the Religious Imagination*. Ed. Dale F. Eickelman and James Piscatori. New York: Routledge, 1990. 50–65.

Ghosh, Amitov. *In an Antique Land*. New York: Knopf, 1993.

Glick, Thomas F. *Islamic and Christian Spain in the Early Middle Ages*. Leiden: Brill, 2005.

– *From Muslim Fortress to Christian Castle: Social and Cultural Change in Medieval Spain*. New York: Manchester University Press, 1995.

Goitein, S.D. *A Mediterranean Society: The Jewish Communities of the Arab World as Portrayed in the Documents of the Cairo Geniza*. Vols. 1, 3, 5. Berkeley: University of California Press, 1978.

– *Jews and Arabs: Their Contacts Through the Ages*. New York: Schocken, 1974.

– *Letters of Medieval Jewish Traders*. Princeton: Princeton University Press, 1973.

Goitein, S.D., and Mordechai Akiva Friedman. *India Traders of the Middle Ages: Documents from the Cairo Geniza ("India Book")*. Leiden: Brill, 2008.

Goldberg, Jessica L. *Trade and Institutions in the Medieval Mediterranean: The Geniza Merchants and Their Business World*. Cambridge: Cambridge University Press, 2012.

Grammatico, Daniele. "El Magreb y al-Andalus: una historia humana entretejida." *Marruecos y España: una historia común. Exposición Teatro Real, Marrakech, 17 de enero – 1 de marzo, 2005*. Granada: Fundación El Legado Andalusí, 2005. 17–29.

Grazia, Margreta de. "The Modern Divide: From Either Side." *Journal of Medieval and Early Modern Studies* 37.3 (2007): 453–67.

Greif, Avner. *Institutions and the Path to the Modern Economy: Lessons from Medieval Trade*. New York: Cambridge University Press, 2006.

Guo, Li. *Commerce, Culture, and Community in a Red Sea Port in the Thirteenth Century: The Arabic Documents from Quseir*. Leiden: Brill, 2004.

Gutas, Dmitri. *Greek Thought, Arabic Culture: The Graeco-Arabic Translation Movement in Baghdad and Early 'Abbasid Society (2nd–4th/8th–10th Centuries)*. New York: Routledge, 1998.

Harley, J.B., and David Woodward, eds. *The History of Cartography*. Vol. 2. Bk. 1. Chicago: University of Chicago Press, 1992.

Harney, Michael. *Kinship and Polity in the* Poema de mio Cid. West Lafayette, IN: Purdue University Press, 1993.

Harvey, L.P. *Islamic Spain, 1250–1500*. Chicago: University of Chicago Press, 1990.

Heck, Gene W. *Charlemagne, Muhammad, and the Arab Roots of Capitalism*. Berlin: De Gruyter, 2006.

Held, David, Anthony McGrew, David Goldblatt, and Jonathan Perraton. *Global Transformations: Politics, Economics, and Culture*. Stanford: Stanford University Press, 1999.

Hodgson, Marshall G.S. "The Role of Islam in World History." *International Journal of Middle East Studies* 1.2 (Apr. 1970): 99–123.

– *The Venture of Islam: Conscience and History in a World Civilization*. Chicago: University of Chicago Press, 1974.

Hourani, Albert Habib. *A History of the Arabic Peoples*. Cambridge: Harvard University Press, 1991.

Ibn Ḥazm al-Andalusī. *El collar de la paloma* (*Ṭawq al-Ḥamāma*). Ed. and trans. Jaime Sánchez Ratia. Madrid: Hiperión, 2009.

Ibn al-Kardabūs. *Historia de al-Andalus (Kitāb al-Iktifā')*. Trans. Felipe Maíllo Salgado. Madrid: Akal, 2008.

Isichei, Elizabeth. *A History of African Societies to 1870*. New York: Cambridge University Press, 1997.

Isidore of Seville. *Etimologías*. Vol. 2. Madrid: Biblioteca de autores cristianos, 1994.

Kardulias, P. Nick. "World-Systems Applications for Understanding the Bronze Age in the Eastern Mediterranean." *Archaic State Interaction: The Eastern Mediterranean in the Bronze Age*. Ed. William A. Parkinson and Michael L. Galaty. Santa Fe: School for Advanced Research Press, 2009. 53–80.

Kea, Ray A. "Expansions and Contractions: World-Historical Change and the Western Sudan World-System (1200/1000 BC–1200/1250 AD)." *Journal of World-Systems Research* 10.3 (fall 2004): 723–816.

Kennedy, Hugh. *Muslim Spain and Portugal: A Political History of Al-Andalus*. New York: Longman, 1996.

Khair, Tabish. "African and Asian Travel Texts in the Light of Europe: An Introduction." *Other Routes: 1500 Years of African and Asian Travel Writing*. Ed. Tabish Khair, Martin Leer, Justin D. Edwards, and Hanna Ziadeh. Bloomington: Indiana University Press, 2005. 1–30.

Kosto, Adam J. "What about Spain? Iberia in the Historiography of Medieval European Feudalism." *Feudalism: New Landscapes of Debate*. Ed. Sverre Bagge, Michael H. Gelting, and Thomas Lindkvist. Turnhout: Brepols, 2011. 135–58.

Kushner, Tony. "A Socialism of the Skin." *The Nation*. 4 July 1994.

LaBianca, Oystein S., and Sandra Arnold Scham. "Introduction: Ancient Network Societies." *Connectivity in Antiquity: Globalization as Long-Term Historical Process*. Ed. Oystein S. LaBianca and Sandra Arnold Scham, London: Equinox, 2006. 1–5.

Ladero Quesada, Miguel Ángel. "Sobre la evolución de las fronteras medievales hispánicas (siglos XI a XIV)." *Identidad y representación de la frontera en la España medieval (siglos XI–XIV)*. Ed. Carlos de Ayala Martínez, Pascal Buresi, and Philippe Josserand. Madrid: Casa de Velázquez, Universidad Autónoma de Madrid, 2001. 3–49.

Lee, Richard E. "The Modern World-System: Its Structures, Its Geoculture, Its Crisis and Transformation." *Immanuel Wallerstein and the Problem of the*

World: System, Scale, Culture. Ed. David Palumbo-Liu, Bruce Robbins, and Nirvana Tanoukhi. Durham: Duke University Press, 2011. 27–40.

Le Goff, Jacques. *Time, Work, and Culture in the Middle Ages*. Trans. Arthur Goldhammer. Chicago: University of Chicago Press, 1980.

Libros españoles de viajes medievales (selección). Ed. Joaquín Rubio Tovar. Madrid: Taurus, 1986.

Linehan, Peter. "At the Spanish Frontier." *The Medieval World*. Ed. Peter Linehan and Janet L. Nelson. New York: Routledge, 2001. 37–59.

Lirola Delgado, Jorge. "El tráfico marítimo de la Almería andalusí (siglos X–XII)." *Almería: "puerta del Mediterráneo" (ss. X–XII)*. Coord. Ángel Suárez Márquez. Sevilla: Junta de Andalucía y Consejería de Cultura, 2007. 99–116.

"Llívia." Wikipedia. es.wikipedia.org/wiki/Llivia.

Loomba, Ania. "Periodization, Race, and Global Contact." *Journal of Medieval and Early Modern Studies* 37.3 (fall 2007): 595–620.

López Alonso, Carmen. *La pobreza en la España medieval: estudio histórico-social*. Madrid: Ministerio de Trabajo y Seguridad Social, 1986.

Lourie, Elena. "The Will of Alfonso I, 'El Batallador,' King of Aragon and Navarre: A Reassessment." *Speculum*, 50.4 (Oct. 1975): 635–51.

Mâle, Emile. *Art religieux du XIIe siècle en France: étude sur les origines de l'iconographie du Moyen Age*. Paris: Armand Colin, 1924.

Manzano Moreno, Eduardo. *Historia de las sociedades musulmanas en la Edad Media*. Madrid: Síntesis, 1992.

– "Christian-Muslim Frontier in Al-Andalus: Idea and Reality." *The Arab Influence in Medieval Europe*. Ed. Dionisius A. Agius and Richard Hitchcock. Reading: Ithaca, 1994. 83–99.

– *Historia de España: épocas medievales*. Vol. 2. Barcelona: Crítica/Marcial Pons, 2010.

– "Prólogo a esta edición." *La formación del feudalismo en la Península Ibérica*. Abilio Barbero and Marcelo Vigil. 2nd ed. Barcelona: Crítica, 2015. vii–xxi.

Maravall, José Antonio. *El concepto de España en la Edad Media*. Madrid: Instituto de Estudios Políticos, 1954.

– *Antiguos y modernos: la idea de progreso en el desarrollo inicial de una sociedad*. Madrid: Sociedad de Estudios y Publicaciones, 1967.

– *Estado moderno y mentalidad social (siglos XV a XVII)*. Vol. 1. Madrid: Revista de Occidente, 1972.

Margariti, Roxani Eleni. *Aden and the Indian Ocean Trade: 150 Years in the Life of a Medieval Arabian Port*. Chapel Hill: University of North Carolina Press, 2007.

Marín, Manuela. *Al-Ándalus y los andalusíes*. Barcelona: CIDOB/Icaria, 2000.

– *Individuo y sociedad en al-Ándalus*. Madrid: Mapfre, 1992.

Márquez Villanueva, Francisco. *El concepto cultural alfonsí*, Barcelona: Bellaterra, 2004.

– *Santiago: trayectoria de un mito*. Barcelona: Bellaterra, 2004.

Martín Corrales, Eloy. *La imagen del magrebí en España: una perspectiva histórica, siglos XVI–XX*. Barcelona: Bellaterra, 2002.

Mattoso, José, coord. *História de Portugal*. Vol. 2. *A Monarquia Feudal (1096–1480)*. Lisbon: Estampa, 1993.

McMillan, M.E. *The Meaning of Mecca: The Politics of Pilgrimage in Early Islam*. London: Saqi, 2011.

Menĕndez Pidal, Ramón. *La España del Cid*. Vol. 1. Madrid: Espasa-Calpe, 1947.

Menocal, María Rosa. *The Arabic Role in Medieval Literary History: A Forgotten Heritage*. Philadelphia: University of Pennsylvania Press, 1987.

– *Writing in Dante's Cult of Truth: From Borges to Boccaccio*. Durham: Duke University Press, 1991.

– *Shards of Love: Exile and the Origins of the Lyric*. Durham: Duke University Press, 1994.

– "Visions of Al-Andalus." *The Literature of Al-Andalus*. Ed. María Rosa Menocal, Raymond P. Scheindlin, and Michael Sells. New York: Cambridge University Press, 2000. 1–24.

– *The Ornament of the World: How Muslims, Jews, and Christians Created a Culture of Tolerance in Medieval Spain*. Boston: Little, Brown, 2002.

– "Why Iberia?" *diacritics* 36.3–4 (fall–winter 2006): 7–11.

Meyerson, Mark D. "Introduction." *Christians, Muslims, and Jews in Medieval and Early Modern Spain: Interaction and Cultural Change*. Notre Dame: University of Notre Dame Press, 2000. xi–xxi.

Mitchell, William J. *Me++: The Cyborg Self and the Networked City*. Cambridge, MA: MIT Press, 2003.

Mitre Fernández, Emilio. "La cristiandad medieval y las formulaciones fronterizas." *Fronteras y fronterizos en la historia*. Ed. Emilio Mitre Fernández, Ricardo García Cárcel, Manuel Lucena Giraldo, Friedrich Edelmeyer, and Borja de Riquer i Permanyer. Valladolid: Instituto de Historia Simancas, Universidad de Valladolid, 1997. 7–62.

Mohammad-Marzouk, Methal R. "Knowledge, Culture, and Positionality: Analysis of Three Medieval Muslim Travel Accounts." *Cross-Cultural Communication* 8.6 (2012): 1–10.

Molina López, Emilio. "El Islam como mundo jurídico: convergencias y divergencias entre Oriente y Occidente." *Al-Andalus y Oriente Medio: pasado y presente de una herencia común*. Ed. Fátima Roldán Castro. Seville: Fundación El Monte, 2006. 63–78.

Mollat, Michel. *The Poor in the Middle Ages: An Essay in Social History*. Trans. Arthur Goldhammer. New Haven: Yale University Press, 1978.

Montaner Frutos, Alberto. "Un canto de frontera: (geopolítica y geopoética del *Cantar de mio Cid*)." *Ínsula* 731 (Nov. 2007): 8–11.

– "*Cantar de mio Cid*." *Dictionary of Literary Biography*. Vol. 337. *Castilian Writers 1200–1400*. Ed. George D. Greenia and Frank A. Dominguez. Detroit: Thomson Gale, 2008. 25–46.

Montes Romero-Camacho, Isabel. "El comercio exterior de cereales en el Reino de Sevilla durante el siglo XV." *La península ibérica entre el Mediterráneo y el Atlántico, siglos XIII–XV*. Ed. Manuel González Jiménez e Isabel Montes Romero-Camacho. Cádiz y Sevilla: Diputación de Cádiz/Sociedad Española de Estudios Medievales, 2006. 111–31.

Netton, Ian Richard. "Preface." *Golden Roads: Migration, Pilgrimage, and Travel in Medieval and Modern Islam*. Ed. Ian Richard Netton. Surrey: Curzon, 1993. x–xv.

Nixon, Sam, Thilo Rehren, Maria Filomena Guerra. "New Light on the Early West African Gold Trade: Coin Moulds from Tadmekka, Mali." *Antiquity* 85 (2011): 1353–68.

Nongbri, Brent. *Before Religion: A History of a Modern Concept*. New Haven: Yale University Press, 2013.

O'Callaghan, Joseph F. *Reconquest and Crusade in Medieval Spain*. Philadelphia: University of Pennsylvania Press, 2003.

O'Fahey, R.S. "Fūr and Fartit: The History of a Frontier." *Culture History in the Southern Sudan: Archaeology, Linguistics, and Ethnohistory*. Ed. John Mack and Peter Robertshaw. Nairobi: British Institute in Eastern Africa, 1982. 75–87.

Ohler, Norbert. *The Medieval Traveller*. Trans. Caroline Hillier. Woodbridge: Boydell, 1989.

Oliver Pérez, Dolores. *El* Cantar de Mío Cid*: génesis y autoría árabe*. Almería: Fundación Ibn Tufayl de Estudios Árabes, 2008.

Osterhammel, Jürgen, and Niels P. Petersson. *Globalization: A Short History*. Princeton: Princeton University Press, 2005.

Other Routes: 1500 Years of African and Asian Travel Writing. Ed. Tabish Khair, Martin Leer, Justin D. Edwards, and Hanna Ziadeh. Bloomington: Indiana University Press, 2005.

Pagden, Anthony. *Lords of All the World: Ideologies of Empire in Spain*. New Haven: Yale University Press, 1995.

Palumbo-Liu, David, Bruce Robbins, and Nirvana Tanoukhi, eds. *Immanuel Wallerstein and the Problem of the World: System, Scale, Culture*. Durham: Duke University Press, 2011.

Palumbo-Liu, David, Bruce Robbins, and Nirvana Tanoukhi. "Introduction: The Most Important Thing Happening." *Immanuel Wallerstein and the*

Problem of the World: System, Scale, Culture. Ed. David Palumbo-Liu, Bruce Robbins, and Nirvana Tanoukhi. Durham: Duke University Press, 2011. 1–23.

Parkinson, William, and Michael L. Galaty. "Introduction: Interaction and Ancient Societies." *Archaic State Interaction: The Eastern Mediterranean in the Bronze Age*. Ed. William A. Parkinson and Michael L. Galaty. Santa Fe: School for Advanced Research Press, 2009. 3–28.

Peirce, Leslie. "An Imperial Caste: Inverted Racialization in the Architecture of Ottoman Sovereignty." *Rereading the Black Legend: The Discourses of Religious and Racial Difference in the Renaissance Empires*. Ed. Maureen Quilligan, Walter Mignolo, and Margaret Rich Greer. Chicago: University of Chicago Press, 2007. 27–47.

Pellat, Ch. "Ibn Ḏjubayr, Abu 'l-Ḥusayn Muḥammad b. Aḥmad b. Ḏjubayr al-Kinānī." *Encyclopedia of Islam, Second Edition*. Ed. P. Bearman, Th. Bianquis, C.E. Bosworth, E. van Donzel, and W.P. Heinrichs. Leiden: Brill Online, 2013.

Penny, Ralph. *History of the Spanish Language*. 2nd ed. New York: Cambridge University Press, 2002.

Phillips, William D., Jr. *Slavery in Medieval and Early Modern Iberia*. Philadelphia: University of Pennsylvania Press, 2014.

Polanyi, Karl. *Primitive, Archaic, and Modern Economies: Essays of Karl Polanyi*. Ed. George Dalton. New York: Doubleday, 1968.

Pym, Anthony. *Negotiating the Frontier: Translators and Intercultures in Hispanic History*. Manchester: St Jerome, 2000.

Rabasa, José. "Decolonizing Medieval Mexico." *Medievalisms in the Postcolonial World: The Idea of "the Middle Ages" Outside Europe*. Ed. Kathleen Davis and Nadia Altschul. Baltimore: Johns Hopkins University Press, 2009. 27–50.

Reynolds, Susan. "Society: Hierarchy and Solidarity." *The Cambridge World History: Expanding Webs of Exchange and Conflict, 500 CE–1500 CE*. Ed. Benjamin Z. Kedar and Merry E. Wiesner-Hanks. Vol. 5. Cambridge: Cambridge University Press, 2015. 94–115.

Robinson, Cynthia. *In Praise of Song: The Making of Courtly Culture in al-Andalus and Provence, 1005–1134 AD*. Leiden: Brill, 2007.

Robson, J. "Ḥadīth." *Encyclopaedia of Islam, Second Edition*. Vol. 3. Ed. P. Bearman, Th. Bianquis, C.E. Bosworth, E. van Donzel, and W.P. Heinrichs. Leiden: Brill, 2010. 23.

Rodríguez Porto, Rosa María. "Courtliness and Its *Trujamanes*: Manufacturing Chivalric Imagery across the Castilian-Grenadine Frontier." *Medieval Encounters* 14 (2008): 219–66.

Roseman, Sharon R., and Shawn S. Parkhurst. "Culture and Space in Iberian Anthropology." *Recasting Culture and Space in Iberian Contexts*. Ed. Sharon

R. Roseman and Shawn S. Parkhurst. Albany: State University of New York Press, 2008. 1–32.

Rouighi, Ramzi. *The Making of a Mediterranean Emirate: Ifrīqiyā and Its Andalusis, 1200–1400*. Philadelphia: University of Pennsylvania Press, 2011.

Ruiz, Teófilo F. *Spanish Society, 1400–1600*. New York: Longman/Pearson, 2001.

– *From Heaven to Earth: The Reordering of Castilian Society, 1150–1350*. Princeton: Princeton University Press, 2004.

Ruggles, D. Fairchild. "Mothers of a Hybrid Dynasty: Race, Genealogy, and Acculturation in al-Andalus." *Journal of Medieval and Early Modern Studies* 34.1 (winter 2004): 65–94.

– "The Geographic and Social Mobility of Slaves: The Rise of Shajar al'Durr, A Slave-Concubine in Thirteenth-Century Egypt." *The Medieval Globe* 2.1 (2016): 41–55.

Russell, P.E. *Spain: A Companion to Spanish Studies*. London: Methuen, 1973.

Ruzafa García, Manuel. "Valencia, puerto mediterráneo y atlántico en el s. XV. Relaciones con Andalucía, reino de Granada y norte de África." *La península ibérica entre el Mediterráneo y el Atlántico, siglos XIII–XV*. Ed. Manuel González Jiménez e Isabel Montes Romero-Camacho. Cádiz y Sevilla: Diputación de Cádiz/Sociedad Española de Estudios Medievales, 2006. 95–101.

Safran, Janina M. *Defining Boundaries in al-Andalus: Muslims, Christians, and Jews in Islamic Iberia*. Ithaca: Cornell University Press, 2013.

Schacht, J. "Aḥkām." *Encyclopaedia of Islam, Second Edition*. Vol. 1. Ed. P. Bearman, Th. Bianquis, C.E. Bosworth, E. van Donzel, and W.P. Heinrichs. Leiden: Brill, 2010. 256.

Schoeler, G., and W. Stoetzer. "Zadjal." *Encyclopedia of Islam, Second Edition*. Ed. P. Bearman, Th. Bianquis, C.E. Bosworth, E. van Donzel, and W.P Heinrichs. Brill Online. 2016.

Sedgwick, Eve Kosofsky. *Between Men: English Literature and Male Homosocial Desire*. New York: Columbia University Press, 1992.

Sénac, Philippe. "Le Maghreb al-Aqsā et l'Occident chrétien (VIIIe–IXe siècles)." *Le Maghreb, al-Andalus et la Méditerranée occidentale (VIIIe–XIIIe siècle)*. Ed. Philippe Sénac. Toulouse: Université de Toulouse-Le Mirail, 2007. 19–36.

– *Los soberanos carolingios y al-Andalus (siglos VIII–IX)*. Trans. Beatriz and María José Molina Rueda. Granada: University of Granada, 2010.

Singh Grewal, David. *Network Power: The Social Dynamics of Globalization*. New Haven: Yale University Press, 2008.

Sourdel, D. "Ghulām." *The Encyclopedia of Islam, Second Edition*. Ed. P. Bearman, Th. Bianquis, C.E. Bosworth, E. van Donzel, W.P. Heinrichs. Brill Online, 2016.

Spaccarelli, Thomas D. *A Medieval Pilgrim's Companion: Reassessing* El libro de los huéspedes *(Escorial MS. h.I.13)*. Chapel Hill: North Carolina Studies in the Romance Languages and Literatures, 1999.

Spiegel, Gabrielle M. *Past as Text: The Theory and Practice of Medieval Historiography*. Baltimore: Johns Hopkins University Press, 1997.

Stiglitz, Joseph E. *Globalization and Its Discontents*. New York: Norton, 2002.

Sublet, Jacqueline. "Nisba." *Encyclopedia of Islam, Second Edition*. Ed. P. Bearman, Th. Bianquis, C.E. Bosworth, E. van Donzel, W.P. Heinrichs. Brill Online, 2016.

Subramanian, Lakshmi. *Medieval Seafarers of India*. New Delhi: Roli, 1999.

Summit, Jennifer, and David Wallace. "Rethinking Periodization." *Journal of Medieval and Early Modern Studies* 37.3 (fall 2007): 447–51.

Sumption, Jonathan. *The Age of Pilgrimage: The Medieval Journey to God*. Mahwah, NJ: Hidden Spring, 2003.

Touati, Houari. *Islam and Travel in the Middle Ages*. Chicago: University of Chicago Press, 2010.

Tuñón de Lara, Manuel. *Historia de España*. Vol. 1. Barcelona: Labor, 1980.

Turner, Frederick Jackson. "The Significance of the Frontier in American History." *Where Cultures Meet: Frontiers in American History*. Ed. David J. Weber and Jane M. Rausch. Wilmington, DE: Scholarly Resources, 1994. 1–50.

Udovitch, Abraham L. "Commercial Techniques in Early Medieval Islamic Trade." *Islam and the Trade of Asia: A Colloquium*. Ed. D.S. Richards. Philadelphia: University of Pennsylvania Press, 1970. 37–62.

– *Partnership and Profit in Medieval Islam*. Princeton: Princeton University Press, 1970.

– "Theory and Practice of Islamic Law: Some Evidence from the Geniza." *Studia Islamica* 32 (1970): 289–303.

Urvoy, Dominique. "Effets pervers du *hajj*, d'après le cas d'al-Andalus." *Golden Roads: Migration, Pilgrimage, and Travel in Medieval and Modern Islam*. Ed. Ian Richard Netton. Surrey: Curzon, 1993. 43–53.

Varisco, Daniel Martin. "Making 'Medieval' Islam Meaningful." *Medieval Encounters* 13 (2007): 385–412.

Vázquez de Parga, Luis, José María Lacarra, and Juan Uría Ríu. *Las peregrinaciones a Santiago de Compostela*. Vol. 1. Madrid: Escuela de Estudios Medievales/CSIC, 1948.

Vernet, Juan. "La ciencia en el Islam y Occidente." *L'Occidente e l'Islam nell'alto medioevo*, vol. 2, 1964. 537–72.

Viguera Molins, María Jesús. "Al-Andalus y oriente: crónica de una historia compartida." *Al-Andalus y Oriente Medio: pasado y presente de una herencia común*. Ed. Fátima Roldán Castro. Sevilla: Fundación El Monte, 2006. 35–62.

Wacks, David. *Framing Iberia: Maqāmāt and Frametale Narratives in Medieval Spain*. Leiden: Brill, 2007.

Wallerstein, Immanuel. *The Modern World System I: Capitalist Agriculture and the Origins of the European World-Economy in the Sixteenth Century*. New York: Academic Press, 1974.

– *Historical Capitalism* with *Capitalist Civilization*. London: Verso, 1983 (2011).

– *World-Systems Analysis: An Introduction*. Durham: Duke University Press, 2004.

– "Thinking about the 'Humanities.'" *Immanuel Wallerstein and the Problem of the World: System, Scale, Culture*. Ed. David Palumbo-Liu, Bruce Robbins, and Nirvana Tanoukhi. Durham: Duke University Press, 2011. 223–6.

Watts, John. *The Making of Polities: Europe, 1300–1500*. New York: Cambridge University Press, 2009.

Webb, Diana. *Medieval European Pilgrimage, c. 700–c.1500*. New York: Palgrave, 2002.

Wensinck, A.J., and B. Lewis. "Hadjdj." *Encyclopedia of Islam, Second Edition*. Ed. P. Bearman, Th. Bianquis, C.E. Bosworth, E. van Donzel, and W.P. Heinrichs. Brill Online, 2011.

Zéraoui, Zidane, and Roberto Marín Guzmán. "Introducción." *Árabes y musulmanes en Europa: historia y procesos migratorios*. Ed. Zidane Zéraoui and Roberto Marín Guzmán. San José: Universidad de Costa Rica, 2006. xvii–xxiv.

Index

TORONTO IBERIC

1 Anthony J. Cascardi, *Cervantes, Literature, and the Discourse of Politics*
2 Jessica A. Boon, *The Mystical Science of the Soul: Medieval Cognition in Bernardino de Laredo's Recollection Method*
3 Susan Byrne, *Law and History in Cervantes' Don Quixote*
4 Mary E. Barnard and Frederick A. de Armas (eds), *Objects of Culture in the Literature of Imperial Spain*
5 Nil Santiáñez, *Topographies of Fascism: Habitus, Space, and Writing in Twentieth-Century Spain*
6 Nelson Orringer, *Lorca in Tune with Falla: Literary and Musical Interludes*
7 Ana M. Gómez-Bravo, *Textual Agency: Writing Culture and Social Networks in Fifteenth-Century Spain*
8 Javier Irigoyen-García, *The Spanish Arcadia: Sheep Herding, Pastoral Discourse, and Ethnicity in Early Modern Spain*
9 Stephanie Sieburth, *Survival Songs: Conchita Piquer's* Coplas *and Franco's Regime of Terror*
10 Christine Arkinstall, *Spanish Female Writers and the Freethinking Press, 1879–1926*
11 Margaret Boyle, *Unruly Women: Performance, Penitence, and Punishment in Early Modern Spain*
12 Evelina Gužauskytė, *Christopher Columbus's Naming in the* diarios *of the Four Voyages (1492–1504): A Discourse of Negotiation*

13 Mary E. Barnard, *Garcilaso de la Vega and the Material Culture of Renaissance Europe*
14 William Viestenz, *By the Grace of God: Francoist Spain and the Sacred Roots of Political Imagination*
15 Michael Scham, Lector Ludens*: The Representation of Games and Play in Cervantes*
16 Stephen Rupp, *Heroic Forms: Cervantes and the Literature of War*
17 Enrique Fernandez, *Anxieties of Interiority and Dissection in Early Modern Spain*
18 Susan Byrne, *Ficino in Spain*
19 Patricia M. Keller, *Ghostly Landscapes: Film, Photography, and the Aesthetics of Haunting in Contemporary Spanish Culture*
20 Carolyn A. Nadeau, *Food Matters: Alonso Quijano's Diet and the Discourse of Food in Early Modern Spain*
21 Cristian Berco, *From Body to Community: Venereal Disease and Society in Baroque Spain*
22 Elizabeth R. Wright, *The Epic of Juan Latino: Dilemmas of Race and Religion in Renaissance Spain*
23 Ryan D. Giles, *Inscribed Power: Amulets and Magic in Early Spanish Literature*
24 Jorge Pérez, *Confessional Cinema: Religion, Film, and Modernity in Spain's Development Years (1960–1975)*
25 Juan Ramon Resina, *Josep Pla: Seeing the World in the Form of Articles*
26 Javier Irigoyen-Garcia, *"Moors Dressed as Moors": Clothing, Social Distinction, and Ethnicity in Early Modern Iberia*
27 Jean Dangler, *Edging toward Iberia*

www.ingramcontent.com/pod-product-compliance
Lightning Source LLC
LaVergne TN
LVHW041113090826
844660LV00062B/891/J

* 9 7 8 1 4 8 7 5 0 1 2 3 5 *